A Wedding with Spirit

A Guide to

Making Your Wedding

(and Marriage)

More Meaningful

GERTRUD MUELLER NELSON

and CHRISTOPHER WITT

Three Leaves Press

Doubleday / New York

A previous edition of this book was published in 1998 by Doubleday under the title *Sacred Threshold: Rituals and Readings for a Wedding with Spirit.*

THREE
LEAVES
PRESS

PUBLISHED BY DOUBLEDAY
a division of Random House, Inc.

THREE LEAVES PRESS and its colophon are trademarks of Random House, Inc., and DOUBLEDAY and its colophon are registered trademarks of Random House, Inc.

Grateful acknowledgment is made for permission to reprint excerpts from the following copyrighted works: "Benediction," copyright 1930 and renewed © 1958 by Stanley Kunitz, from *The Poems of Stanley Kunitz 1928–1978* by Stanley Kunitz, reprinted by permission of W.W. Norton & Company, Inc.; excerpt from "The Country of Marriage" in *The Country of Marriage,* copyright © 1971 by Wendell Berry, reprinted by permission of Harcourt Brace & Company; excerpt from *100 Poems from the Japanese* by Kenneth Rexroth, copyright © 1955 by New Directions Publishing Corp., reprinted by permission of New Directions Publishing Corp.; excerpts from the English translation of *Rite of Marriage,* © 1969, International Committee on English in the Liturgy, Inc., all rights reserved; "The Love of God . . ." by Dante, transl. by S. Mitchell, from *The Enlightened Heart* by Stephen Mitchell, copyright © 1989 by Stephen Mitchell, reprinted by permission of HarperCollins Publishers, Inc.; "Sonnet XVII" by Pablo Neruda, transl. by S. Mitchell from *Into the Garden: A Wedding Anthology* by Robert Hass and Stephen Mitchell, reprinted by permission of HarperCollins Publishers, Inc.

The Library of Congress has cataloged the Image edition as follows:

Nelson, Gertrud Mueller.
Sacred threshold : rituals and readings for a wedding with spirit / by Gertrud Mueller Nelson and Christopher Witt. — 1st ed.
p. cm.
"Image books."
1. Wedding etiquette. 2. Wedding—Planning. I. Witt, Christopher, 1951– . II. Title.
BJ2051.N379 1998
395.2′2—dc21   97-37656
                                                                          CIP

ISBN 0-385-51789-0

PRINTED IN THE UNITED STATES OF AMERICA

February 2006

First Three Leaves Press Edition
10 9 8 7 6 5 4 3 2 1

Our thanks to the many people who shared
their stories with us for this book.

G.M.N. AND C.W.

This union, then, is most sacred and most serious,

because it will bind you together for life

in a relationship so close and so intimate

that it will profoundly influence your whole future.

That future, with its hopes and disappointments,

its successes and its failures,

its pleasures and its pains,

its joys and its sorrows, is hidden from your eyes.

You know that these elements are mingled in every life

and are to be expected in your own.

And so, not knowing what is before you,

you take each other for better or for worse,

for richer or for poorer,

in sickness and in health,

until death.

CONTENTS

A Wedding
with Spirit

1

Marriage Is a Threshold

For Now and Always

We are happy you have chosen this book. Unlike other wedding books, this one is for both of you, not just for the bride. As a society we are just beginning to appreciate and honor the equality of man and woman in marriage. It is time that weddings reflect this equality, not only by eliminating or altering those parts of the ceremony that slight a woman's dignity but also by encouraging the man's participation in planning and in being fully part of the celebration itself.

We also wrote this book for people who are searching for something *more* for their wedding. Not more as in bigger, grander, or more lavish, but more as in more meaningful, gracious, and sacred.

We approach a wedding less as a production to be orchestrated according to a complex and often outdated etiquette and more as a public celebration of a personal commitment, an event that is social and intimate, holy and joyful. The most successful weddings, to our way of thinking, are marked by hospitality, graciousness, and inclusivity. Wedding celebrations "work" when everyone present feels brought together—even bound together—in an active, holy, and deeply satisfying undertaking.

This book builds on these basic assumptions:

- *A wedding is for a day, a marriage lasts a lifetime.*
- *A wedding is a spiritual event, a sacred threshold to a new life together.*
- *A wedding is a ritual celebrated by a community.*

A Lifelong Marriage

Your wedding is important and will certainly give you a lifetime of memories. Planning it deserves your full attention. But instead of trying to orchestrate "the happiest day of your life," see your wedding as a moment in the larger context of your love. Make it reflect your love for each other, your shared dreams and hopes.

Planning a wedding is a major undertaking that requires months of planning, consulting, negotiating, shopping, and socializing. In some parts of the country it is necessary to reserve the church, the reception hall, the caterer, musicians, and photographers a year or more in advance. Bridal magazines and wedding planners publish checklists that take into account every detail you need to address over the coming months. We suggest that you use them in conjunction with this book, but we recognize at the same time how daunting they can make the whole wedding seem. The details that rightly demand attention can also overwhelm you and make you lose touch with each other and with the very reason for your efforts. The details can also draw your attention away from the greater task, the hard and joyful work of making a deep and loving marriage.

We wrote this book convinced that it is possible to plan and celebrate a wedding in a way that both reflects and enriches your love. We address the quality of your preparations and the ceremony itself. We offer for your consideration the spirit, attitudes, concerns, and values you bring to bear in the planning. We are, frankly, less concerned that you finesse the "perfect wedding" (something unexpected always happens) than that you marry with grace and graciousness. For your wedding day is meant to send you on your way together into a new life—into a loving, life-enhancing marriage.

Remind yourselves, when feeling overwhelmed, that a wedding is for a day, marriage for a lifetime.

A Spiritual Event

Marriage is caught up in the mystery of God. All major faith traditions consider marriage holy. They recognize something sacred about the committed love between two people, about love's ability to create and nurture life, about the faithfulness and hope that such a love gives witness to. For this reason, all major religions mark the beginning of marriage with rich communal rituals.

For Christians marriage is indeed holy.

The Orthodox and Catholic churches teach that it is one of the seven sacraments, a sign of God's presence in the world and a means of grace.

IN THE JEWISH TRADITION, a wedding is much more than the joining of two people or even two families. It is a celebration for the entire community and for God. The central symbol of the wedding ceremony, the canopy, represents the ideal home, which the couple enters at the beginning of the wedding ceremony, escorted by their parents. Traditionally, close friends or family members hold the canopy's poles, to symbolize the support that others pledge to the couple throughout their lives together. The canopy, a home without walls, calls to mind the presence of the *Shechinah,* the protecting presence of God.

IN BURMA, Buddhists begin their wedding day by hosting a special meal in the bride's house for the village monks. During their wedding ceremony at the local shrine their hands are held together and immersed in a bowl of water to make "their union as indivisible as water."

HINDU WEDDING CEREMONIES differ from region to region and for each different caste in India, but there are certain essential elements common to them all. The wedding date is fixed only after careful astrological calculations have been made. The bridegroom is conducted to the home of his future parents-in-law, who receive him as an honored guest. After the parents and the couple make offerings to the fire, the groom takes his bride by the hand and leads her around this sacrificial fire. They take seven steps together to solemnize their irrevocable unity. Then both are conducted to their new home, which the bride enters without touching the threshold.

The Episcopal Book of Common Prayer says: "The union of husband and wife in heart, body, and mind is intended by God for their mutual joy, for the help and comfort given one another in prosperity and adversity, and, when it is God's will, for the procreation of children and their nurture in the knowledge and love of the Lord."

The minister's instruction at the beginning of the Lutheran marriage ceremony states: "The Lord God in his goodness created us male and female, and by the gift of marriage founded human community in a joy that begins now and is brought to perfection in the life to come."

A Quaker man and woman marry at a public gathering, where they declare their commitment to each other without the services of a minister. They believe that God alone makes a couple husband and wife.

Although each church has its own ritual for celebrating and blessing the marriage of its members, they are amazingly similar.

————

Perhaps you aren't presently involved with a particular church. It could be that you drifted away from the religious community of your childhood and got caught up in other issues and concerns. Although you haven't thought about religion, you may still feel a connection with something you vaguely feel as spirituality. Maybe you can't articulate what you believe about God or faith or religion. Perhaps you don't even understand why, when you think about your wedding, you are naturally drawn to a spiritual wedding, whether in a church or outside a church. That's fine. This book isn't about converting or convincing you to join a religion. Rather, it asks you to be open to mystery, to the possibility that God is gracious and desires your mutual happiness and well-being. We hope this book will help you appreciate the rituals of whatever church you feel connected to and experience the presence and blessings of God in and through your wedding ceremony. And if, for whatever reason, you decide not to be married in a church, we hope this book will help you create a ceremony grounded in the sacred and in your own spiritual sensibilities.

A Sacred Ritual

Life is filled with ritual. Thanksgiving dinner with family and friends, turkey, and all the trimmings is a ritual. A birthday party with a cake and candles, with singing, and a wish is a ritual. Certainly a wedding with its special attire, with processions, music, vows, and the exchange of rings is a ritual.

Ritual is what brings people together in community. It unites us in a physical place and time and on a deeper level binds us together in a common undertaking. Ritual uses traditional elements and actions to create a safe passage for the central participants, that they might pass from one state of being to a new one.

Throughout this book we discuss a variety of customs, actions, and gestures you can employ to gather your families and guests into a community. Most of these customs are drawn from Christian traditions. We help you reclaim traditions of substance, reframe customs that have lost their value, and discard trivial or demeaning practices. We suggest ways you can involve your guests in celebrating with you, in witnessing your commitment, and in surrounding you with their blessings and love.

The Wedding Industry

To create the wedding both of you hope for, you may enlist the services of a small army of professionals—caterers, florists, photographers, seamstresses, printers, bakers, janitors, deejays, and musicians. Many professionals are committed to providing a necessary and helpful service, although there are some who profit by catering to an engaged couple's insecurities. They create false needs and pander to a couple's desire to do "the right thing." Throughout this book we call them "the wedding industry," and we suggest ways you can reduce your reliance on them.

Distrust anyone who offers you a product or service, saying, "You deserve the best" or "This is your special day" or "It happens only once in a lifetime" or "A wedding would be incomplete without this." They are making a thinly disguised sales pitch. Unless you approach such professionals with common sense and with your own values clearly in mind, you can easily exhaust your savings and forgo the down payment on a fair-sized house.

You *do* deserve the best—which has little to do with what money can buy. You deserve the fondest support, the dearest expressions of love that family and friends can provide. You deserve the blessings of God. It is your special day—a special day for you both—but it is also a special day in the lives of everyone who loves you. And it can be perfect—not flawless, but perfectly wonderful, right, true, joyful—as perfect as our less-than-perfect world allows. And its perfection is nothing you pay for but exists because of who you are as a couple and because of the Spirit you invite to the wedding.

The Book's Format

The next five chapters discuss the general principles of a wedding. "Crossing the Threshold" introduces the overriding metaphor of this book, while the following chapters reflect on the place, people, symbols, and music of a wedding.

The second section, "The Ceremony and the Reception," moves step by step through the ceremony itself. It focuses on the gathering rite (welcoming your guests, the procession, and the opening prayer), the readings and instruction, the wedding ritual itself (the vows, rings, and blessing). The section concludes with the reception, since it is a social recapitulation of the religious ceremony.

"Matters of Hospitality" deals with the practicalities of invitations, the rehearsal, instructions you can give to your readers, and models for a printed program.

"Making a Marriage" is a collection of meditations—preparing for marriage, dealing with doubts and jitters, exploring dimensions of marriage in the Bible, and praying.

Finally, "Making the Day: Examples" describes three different weddings.

———

May your wedding—this crossing of the threshold—be a step into the sacred. May the hand of the holy one who leads you bless and protect you all the days of your life.

Crossing the Threshold

Once upon a time, and not so long ago at that, it was customary for a man to carry his bride over the threshold into his house. The custom, an outward sign of a couple's entry into marriage, is preserved today more in memory than in observance.

Some trace the practice to ancient Rome, where a day of wedding festivities ended at night with a procession. With torches blazing and to the accompaniment of music and singing, the groom's friends escorted the bride to her husband's house, where the entry had been festooned with garlands of flowers in preparation for her arrival. There the married men—those still sober enough to do so—lifted the bride and carried her over the threshold of the groom's doorway into his house.

This Roman custom may, in turn, be a relic of a still more ancient, more primitive practice, when a man quite literally "took a bride." Those were times when a man may have captured a woman, sometimes from a neighboring tribe, and dragged her forcibly into his house. Or the Roman custom may have reflected some early religious beliefs. Many ancient peoples believed that each place had its own attendant spirit. Spirits resided in mountains and lakes, in fields and forests. They lived in the rocks and in crops. They had their place in barns and sheds and households, where they lurked in the rafters or stood guard at the doorsill. Anyone who ignored the spirits of a place ran the risk of offending them and incurring their wrath. The spirits that haunted the threshold were especially powerful, and people believed that stumbling or treading on them through ignorance or preoccupation brought bad luck. Therefore, to make sure the bride didn't trip up and begin her marriage on a wrong footing, she was carried over the threshold in safety.

Today few of us accept the notion that a man takes possession of his wife or, for that matter, that she needs his protection against the impish spirits that lie in wait around doorways. Through gradual disuse more than by conscious consensus, we have allowed the custom to die out slowly. It is a rare groom who carries his bride over the threshold on their wedding night. And yet, even as we reject the custom's superstitious and sexist implications, we can still discover in it a deeper kernel of value. Old practices often express a symbolic truth.

A Wedding Is a Threshold

When you marry, you make a transition. You step over a threshold, crossing from one way of life to another, from being single to being married. You walk across the threshold, not one of you carrying the other, but hand in hand, as equals and as two persons in mutual support. You enter a whole new way of relating to each other and assume an entirely new position in the society around you.

At the threshold of your wedding you step away from what is familiar and predictable and enter a place you have never been before. This transition is like and unlike other thresholds you have already crossed—being born, entering adolescence, graduating, starting a new job—and ones you may yet encounter—giving birth, raising a family, growing old, retiring, dying—in that you have no way of knowing beforehand where you will end up or what you will experience on the other side. In a sense, your wedding is a passage that takes you from the comfortably familiar into a place of mystery. In crossing, you almost hover and are not yet here or there. You step into a time that will leave you feeling disoriented and out of control. You will take on new roles and identities. You will no longer be "your own person," free to do as you please. No longer simply your parents' child, you will be, after a brief ceremony, husband and wife. For as often as you have seen marriage played out by others, or imagined yourselves as married, you don't actually know what married life will be like for you. Even if you have been married before, you still don't know what *this* marriage will hold for you.

Small wonder, as you approach this threshold where things are strange and untried, you suddenly feel vulnerable, tender, and exposed. Like a creature that has shed its outgrown shell and waits for its new, soft shell to harden, you become defensive, self-protective, and snappish. Or think of yourself as the adolescent you once were, no longer a child but not yet an adult, ill at ease in your new body and prone to unpredictable moods and responses. Sometimes you returned to your childish ways and sought comfort in the familiar, only to be chided for not growing up. Then you strove for the privileges of the adult and felt unnerved, uncertain, out of step, and sometimes rudely rebuffed. Threshold experiences bewilder and disorient us.

And there, in our vulnerability and bewilderment, the threshold spirits lie in wait, ready to haunt us, demanding attention.

Psychologists who might chuckle at talk of "threshold spirits" would be quite content to warn of the "unresolved conflicts," "neurotic tendencies," or "dependency needs" that surface as people move through a "life transition." You will find—if you haven't already—that wedding preparations raise issues which you thought had been resolved long ago but which now clamor annoyingly for more attention: feelings, fears, relationship problems, and parts of your own personalities you would prefer to ignore or deny.

As though this were not enough to deal with, other people's spirits or neurotic tendencies will also be awakened. Your transition affects everyone around you. As you shift and move, you change a collective balance and force others to reposition themselves. They jostle for equilibrium. They are forced, sometimes against their wills, to shift into their own transitions, to reexamine their roles in your lives, and to recreate a new way of relating to you. Your wedding rustles the status quo and wakes the sleeping spirits of everyone's fears and unfinished business. Friends surprise you by unexpected reactions. Siblings remember past hurts, make childish demands, jockey for attention. Parents withdraw or elbow in to take total control.

Whether you call them threshold spirits, neurosis, or invitations to growth, they do invite everyone to pay attention, or to work through their personal patches of unfinished business. In the meantime, you can count on being tripped up by more than you expected.

Feeling Haunted

When the two of you, deeply in love and bursting with the excitement of your decision to marry, announce the good news to the people you love, you may be taken aback or even hurt by the reaction. They may not respond to your happiness with the unqualified joy and support you expect. The prickly spirits of negativity let loose hurtful or thoughtless comments:

"Isn't this a bit sudden?" or "It's about time!"

"Oh, honey, why *her*?"

"Are you sure you know what you're getting into?"

"Aren't you a bit *young*?" or "Well, finally!"

"So what do you think you'll live on?"

"You two are so—so *different*! How are you ever going to agree on anything?"

Some people may make even more cutting comments behind your back, comments others will "kindly" share with you:

"I liked her other boyfriend so much better."

"Frankly, he's marrying beneath himself."

"Well, we know who's going to wear the pants in that marriage!"

"To be honest, I think she's marrying on the rebound."

"She's such a spirited woman, and he's so, well, I hate to say it, so boring! Oh, well, they say opposites attract!"

Unwelcome Advice

Then there are the spirits of well-meaning but awkward or unwanted advice.

"You *will* be married in a church, won't you?"

"You've been *living* together—you can't get married in a church!"

"Better think pink! And not horrify Grandma by wearing white!"

"Oh, don't have a dinky little wedding. Your mother was so looking forward to going the whole nine yards."

"Oh, gawd! knowing you, this will mean casts of thousands!"

"Listen, kids, if I were you, I'd elope."

Regression

Those were the spirits you stirred up in everyone else. Your own spirits will also rise up and trip you if you are careless. There is the spirit of regression—a common response to the temporary madness transitions unleash. Whenever we are confronted by unfamiliar situations, we tend to revert to less mature ways of behaving. As children, we returned, in times of crisis, to thumb sucking, the bottle, bed wetting, baby talk, or tantrums. As adults we develop more sophisticated, though not always healthier, forms of regression. Drinking. Picking arguments. Getting moody or touchy. Pouting.

Demanding. Being needy or greedy. Being unable to sleep. Breaking out in pimples or hives. Feeling awkward and clutzy. Having a bad-hair-day fit. Losing patience and acting out. The list goes on and you can probably add to it.

Control, Withdrawal, Denial, Neediness

The need to control everything and everyone is a common threshold spirit. So is the fear of being controlled. There are, of course, lists to check off, schedules to keep, and decisions to make, but if you find yourselves becoming picky, obsessed, perfectionistic, bossy, neurotically concerned about minutiae, short-tempered when things don't go your way, then suspect you have unwittingly tripped over the controlling spirits. Or if you find yourself opposing every suggestion and resisting and resenting everything that's going on, you may have stumbled over the spirit that dreads being controlled.

It is helpful to know when and how to take time out to be alone, to relax, and to renew yourselves. It is less helpful—and less healthy—to pull away from each other physically or emotionally. Many people tend to avoid situations that frighten or irritate them. They may avoid the situation altogether, or they may be physically present but emotionally distant. They may agree to do something, but when the time comes they withdraw behind the protective shield of a newspaper or the game on TV. Their withdrawal—physical or emotional—sets off other people's insecurities and fears.

When you get together to do something, agree to be fully present to each other and to what you are doing. Avoid letting

I LOST IT in the housewares department. We had spent the previous afternoon at the florist's. Bad enough. But the next day we started out bright and early with her mom to pick out china, stemware, tablecloths, bed linens. Vases! Then we registered for toasters, mixers, pots and pans, tea towels, and even the stupid measuring cups! At one point I knew that if I heard one more "Honey, look at this" or "Honey, what do you think, pink or green?" or "Honey, what about . . ." I was going to lose it. Well, truth be told, I did lose it—completely lost my cool. I threw an all-out overload tantrum right there in public. I told off her mom and I told my startled bride I didn't give a rat's ass about the color of our dish towels and I didn't know what all this had to do with marriage and as far as I was concerned, we should have eloped a year ago! I may as well have thrown myself on the floor and kicked and howled like a two-year-old! They were so shocked at my behavior, they just gawked at me. Actually, I was shocked listening to myself. There was only one thing left to do: laugh! Thank God we laughed. And took a coffee break. Then they lovingly dismissed me for the rest of the day.

yourselves get distracted or prolonging the task so that it becomes an ordeal. Agree to limits on any project. Divide the tasks according to your interests, talents, and abilities. A man whose eyes glaze over at the thought of shopping, for instance, shouldn't be subjected to unending hours in the stores. Nor should a woman feel stuck with all the details and be given little support.

Denial is a threshold spirit especially fond of tripping up men. While brides tend to get flustered and out of sorts on and off for months before the wedding, men often act as if "it's no big deal." They can look cool, unruffled, and slightly detached, causing their fiancées to wonder if they care at all about what's happen-

ONE BRIDE went into a panic when she learned that with less than twenty-five minutes to go, her fiancé hadn't yet arrived at the church. When he finally showed up with wet hair, he explained that he had gone for a quick surf with his buddies "to kill time and get out of the way."

ing. Usually, they are simply detaching themselves from the stresses of the wedding and from the emotional ups and downs they might otherwise find difficult to handle.

More often than not, the bride, having already engaged a whole range of feelings for weeks on end, finally stands at the start of the wedding procession, calm, serene, and present to the moment. And the groom, who has been fighting off feelings through denial and distractions during the past weeks, suddenly waits at the start of the ceremony looking pale and shaken, overcome with the magnitude of what he is about to undertake.

———

Insecurity, neediness, and emotional vulnerabilities are also common threshold spirits. The wedding industry often plays off these spirits to trip you up. If you doubt yourselves and your own values, you can fall prey to the magazines and the vendors who staff the booths at bridal fairs. They will put ideas into your heads, up-end your values, and convince you that anything simple and wholesome is inadequate. Women, the bride and the bride's mother, are especially at risk.

The spirits that lurk at the threshold of your marriage aren't necessarily evil spirits lying in wait to trip you up. They are your own spiritual issues that demand attention. They are the unnamed shadows of your soul's work-in-progress.

Psychologists say that to acknowledge and accept what you have disowned in yourselves begins the healing process of integration. Folk wisdom says if you name your own dark forces and welcome them, they will bless you in return.

When you find yourselves arguing about something with more intensity than the issue deserves, or when you become "too busy" or withdrawn or vaguely out of sorts for no apparent reason, pay attention. Suspect that one of your spirits has raised its head and demands attention. Name this spirit—name what you feel. Address your feelings directly and honestly. Avoid the temptation to ignore it, for if you do, it will return at another, less convenient time to haunt you. Slow down and say to yourself, "This, too, is part of what I bring to this marriage. This is part of me and this spirit and I can work together."

WHEN I WAS A LITTLE GIRL, I used to dress up my dolls as brides and princesses and get lost in these fairy-tale fantasies. There was always a lot of energy in the magic of veils and long dresses. When I began to leaf through the bridal books and magazines, I thought, hey! These guys know about that energy in little girls! Where do I draw the line between me as a real woman about to make an important life choice and me as a Barbie doll or a little kid playing dress-up!

A Means of Grace

There are, of course, good things that happen at your wedding. People go out of their way to be kind. Families pull together. Friends renew their bonds of affection. Strangers are generous. Chance encounters, unplanned events, and "coincidences" work in your favor. Not every spirit that lurks at the threshold is evil or irksome. As a matter of fact, one Spirit in particular has another purpose in mind.

As you step beyond the limits of what you understand, you lose the illusion of being in control. You take a step—no, a leap—into the unknown. (Maybe that's why we speak of marriage as "taking the plunge.") And instead of falling flat on your faces, you find yourselves lifted up. Airborne even. You sense more than know that being in control is illusory and unnecessary. Being in love, after all, can't be controlled, manipulated, or planned. It is grace.

In nontheological terms, grace is love working in your favor. More than that, grace is *freely given* love working in your favor. It has already been at work in your lives, already begun transforming you. How else could you understand the mystery of your love or the miracle that brought the two of you together?

Grace is another name for what Christians call the Holy Spirit or, simply, the Spirit. As much as we have spoken of the spirits that haunt the threshold of a wedding, we are even more aware of the Spirit that stands there with blessings in hand.

Religious traditions around the world, aware of the Spirit present during transitions, have developed customs to mark the place and the moment of change. They mark the place of a transition—doorways, for example—with blessings. And they mark the moments of transition—birth, adolescence, death, and, of course, weddings—with rituals. Every major spiritual tradition has developed more or less elaborate rituals to celebrate weddings.

A good ritual helps those who participate in it to be conscious of the spirits that would otherwise torment them. And it provides a way of inviting the Holy Spirit in. A good ceremony makes a wedding a threshold into grace.

The Leap

Sometimes a threshold—and the marriage threshold is one of them—is a broad step. It covers a great distance and takes time to cross. Your wedding ceremony may take no more than an hour by the clock, but your entry into marriage is less clearly measured. Your threshold experience began when you first discussed marriage and became engaged, and it will certainly con-

---

OBSERVANT JEWS hang a mezuzah, a piece of sacred Scripture, on their doorways. In parts of India, Hindu women make fresh, fragile rice-flour designs on their outer doorsteps each morning. Shintos in Japan hang a graceful silk or linen *noren* from the lintel—a short curtain that brushes the head and parts as a person passes from one room to the next. In Thailand, Buddhists are careful to step over thresholds out of respect for the attending spirits. In many Christian churches, holy water stands in a font near the entry to remind worshipers that they first entered the church through the waters of baptism. In parts of Europe, Christians bless their homes on the Feast of the Epiphany (the twelfth day of Christmas) by marking their door lintels with a chalked blessing.

---

tinue through the first year of your marriage. Part of the threshold you cross, then, has to do with clock and calendar time. But its spiritual aspect is beyond clock or calendar. It is a time out of time. In German the wedding is called the *Hochzeit,* literally meaning a high time—a time elevated and lifted right out of the ordinary. It is that airborne leap that leaves you no longer here, and not yet there. It is as if this wedding experience lifts you up out of the day-to-day flow of events and places you in a special, a sacred place. A place outside of time.

Clock Time and God's Time

The ancient Greeks recognized two completely different experiences of time.

They spoke of the common passage of time as *chronos.* They meant the chronology of measured time that can be divided into hours and days, and subdivided down to the nanosecond. When you fill the pages of your appointment calendar with meetings, engagements, and dinners, you are engaging *chronos.*

The other sort of time the Greeks recognized is the unmeasurable time that can't be neatly dissected or programmed. It is timeless. The Greek word for this elusive sort of time is *kairos.* You experience it on those occasions when you are so caught up in a situation that you lose all track of time. You know it when you are engrossed in a work that engages your full attention and creativity. You know it when the two of you are lost in each other's love, so totally present to each other and to the moment that later you find yourselves wondering where the time went. The time that expands or contracts depending on your involvement with what you are doing—the time that lifts you out of the ordinary and makes the simplest gestures or words extraordinary—is *kairos.*

Your wedding will plunge you into both *chronos* and *kairos* time.

Because *chronos* plays such an important role in planning your wedding, it gets the larger share of your attention. You have to attend to schedules, calendars, and appointments. You have to coordinate and juggle untold meetings, decisions, and events. The caterer has to arrive at the right place at the right time. So does the florist. Planes have to be met and guests put up. There are fittings and photos, the printer and the musicians to schedule. Failing to attend to the demands of *chronos* lands you in a terrible muddle. But the spontaneous moments and encounters that will make your crossing over into marriage memorable can't be planned or scheduled; they can only be anticipated. The rituals of a wedding are a way of making room in your expectations and in the business of your plans for those special gifts that can be bestowed only by the graces of *kairos.*

Kairos is another name for grace. It is what happens to time when the Spirit enters in with blessing.

During the threshold moments of our lives, we need ceremonies and rituals to shore us up and protect us. We need the wisdom of the ages that lies at the root of these practices to help us cross over in safety. We attend to the spirits that insert themselves into our journey and see them as invitations to engage the gravity of the moment, to engage where we came from and where we hope to go. In full awareness and without fussy sentimentality we name and accept the positive and negative sides of our decisions so as to be standing in a whole truth. We allow both sides of the threshold to meet in the middle to delineate

I THOUGHT I WANTED THE PERFECT WEDDING. I'm a superorganized person, so I set about planning with notebooks, lists, and calendars. The details worked out pretty well with only a very few glitches. In fact, people still talk about what a great celebration we had. But the funny thing is, what I treasure were the little surprises that just dropped from the sky like gifts. I couldn't have planned them. Like my husband's ninety-two-year-old Italian grandmother who brought candied almonds to the rehearsal dinner and captivated us with her stories. She was so touchingly beautiful and wise! Or my mom—on the morning of the wedding she brought me a tiny medal I'd worn when I was baptized that her dad had given her when she was a girl. She pinned it to my slip and told me how much she loved me and how proud she was of me. We bawled. And the way my dad—my always-in-full-control dad—kept blowing his nose into his handkerchief because the words of the readings were so moving—we were all so touched at hearing them, as though we'd never heard them before!

clearly what stays outside and what comes across with us, wanted or not. During the threshold moments of life we feel, we engage feelings, we celebrate in order to engage and elicit feelings. We do this so we know in our very bones that something profound is happening. Most of all, when we stand at the threshold of marriage, we need a ceremony to invite and welcome that sacred Spirit who will bless our transition and in whom our commitment is anchored and our love grounded.

Sacred Space

One of the earliest and most important decisions you have to make is to choose the physical setting for the wedding. Although most couples—almost eighty-five percent—marry in a church, many others decide on different settings: a family member's home or garden, a hotel banquet hall, a park, the forest, or a meadow. Since the place determines so much about the tone and feel of your wedding, its basic spirit, you will want to give it considerable thought. Your attitudes about religion and church, your experiences and personal beliefs, will all come into play as you discuss your options.

You may be actively, faithfully involved in a church. You may be adamantly opposed to any religious organization. Or you may be somewhere in between: You haven't thought much about religion since leaving high school and now, when an important event comes up in your life, you're not altogether sure what you believe or want from a church.

Actively Involved in a Church

If you are an active participant in a church, you won't spend much time thinking about where you want to marry; you already know. You probably even know the priest or minister you want to preside at the ceremony.

A YOUNG WOMAN moved from the Midwest to the West Coast to attend graduate school. There she joined the church connected with the Catholic campus ministry. Over time she became more and more active, first as a volunteer, then as a full-time intern in campus ministry. At one of the weekly student dinners she met another student who was becoming active in the church again after being away for several years. They fell in love and, a year and a half later, decided to marry. On the day of their wedding, people and energy and excitement filled the church. It was packed with family and friends and the many students and faculty who came to know them through the campus ministry. Everyone seated in the pews had a part in the wedding. Everyone knew the music the couple had chosen and sang their hearts out.

"We never thought of marrying anyplace else," said the bride. "The church had been part of who we were and what we believed. This place and this community are part of our identity."

Formerly Involved in a Church

Perhaps you were raised in a church and received religious instruction as a child, and you may still think of yourself as Catholic or Lutheran or Baptist. But like so many young adults, you stopped "practicing the faith" when you left your parents' home. Now, as you consider where to celebrate your wedding, you promptly think of the church you felt connected to. You may not be able to articulate a reason for this inclination. You don't know exactly why you're drawn back to a church you haven't been involved with for years. Perhaps you just feel some deep, inexplicable pull that draws you back: You just always thought of your wedding day as an important spiritual moment, and church is the place where these holy things are celebrated.

So you visit the priest or minister and you are surprised—or frustrated—to find your reasons for wanting to marry in the church questioned. "Where did you say you worship? If you haven't been coming to church all along, why do you come now? Why this church? What makes you want to marry here?" You may even be refused the performance of the ceremony or the use of the church, depending on the particular church's policy or on your own convictions.

Many churches have tightened their policies about weddings. They believe that a church ceremony makes sense only for those who are already committed to the church. Also, priests or ministers who agree to perform a wedding take on a substantial time commitment. They will spend five to ten hours on premarital counseling, two more hours for a rehearsal, and at least that much for the wedding itself. Before they are willing to give so

I WAS RAISED EPISCOPALIAN and though I stopped going to church when I went to college, it never really left my system. I went to services on Christmas and Easter or when I was home visiting my folks. I know. Not exactly what you'd call an active churchgoer or an exemplary Christian. But I've always considered myself a Christian, particularly an Episcopalian. It's just part of me. I believe what the church taught me about marriage. You know, about its being for life and everything. And that it's a holy endeavor, something God is a part of and something we, in turn, need God to be part of. I want us to be married in the church. It's important to us both to have the church's blessing.

The rector agreed to witness the marriage of the young man and his fiancée. "I know other priests in this diocese," she explained, "who would have turned them down. But when a couple comes to me about their wedding, I see it as a moment of grace. Maybe even of spreading the gospel. So many young folks have been alienated from church. How much can we err by being inclusive? I talk to them about how God loves them and delights in their love for each other. How their love is a sharing in God's own love, especially of Christ's love for the Church. And I tell them that the Church is happy to bless their union. One day if they get into trouble, who knows, maybe they'll know where to come."

IN A CERTAIN BAPTIST CHURCH that is very popular with young couples wanting to marry, the pastor likens himself to a lawyer. If you want him to perform your wedding, he asks for a retainer. He regards the down payment as a sign of your commitment. You must then appear for six sessions of premarital counseling, which he maintains any responsible minister would require. If you fail to show up, you pay anyway. The rehearsal and the ceremony itself are then open to your offering. Hard-nosed? Couples come to him in droves.

much time to you, they usually want to know more about the two of you.

No Church Involvement

Perhaps you never had a consistent connection with any church as you grew up, and you are not currently involved with one. You may shy away from describing yourselves as believers in any formal way, yet you speak generally about believing in God and leading a moral life. As you formulate your wedding plans, you may be surprised to find yourselves wanting something that looks like a "church wedding."

Church as a Holy Place

A church is a natural container for sacred functions, built and consecrated as a gathering space for the faithful to pray and worship. Its appointments and architecture, the very walls and windows, all define it as a sacred space—a place set apart.

If you marry in a church, you rarely have to do much to make it suitable for the wedding. You may want to bring in some decorations—flowers, candles, or banners—to add a festive feeling, but it is better to remain elegant and simple. Whatever you bring in should be in keeping and scale with the space, a complement and not a distraction. Remind yourselves—and any overeager florist—that the church is the sacred housing of your ceremony, not a stage, and that the action of the marriage should be the focus of attention.

The church very probably has a policy about flowers—how many arrangements or where they may be placed. Perhaps they

ONE COUPLE wanting to marry had no formal church upbringing. She called herself Christian, although she had no memory of attending church past age eleven. He disliked labels and thought that the essence of any authentic spirituality was being a good person. She said she always dreamed of getting married in a church. She wanted to process down an aisle with the organ blaring the "Wedding March" and to exchange vows in front of a minister with the pews filled with people.

They knew they would feel out of place in a big church. They looked in the yellow pages under wedding chapels and found churches and ministers who specialized in weddings, but they were put off by what they called the commercialization of it all. They attended a friend's wedding and liked the minister who performed it. When they approached him after the service to ask him if he would perform theirs, he agreed to meet with them. He took time to listen to them. They met with him five times to talk about their relationship, about marriage, and about the wedding plans. "He talked about God and God's love in a way that made sense to us," the bride said. "He would have married us at my mother's house if we had wanted, but I wanted to be married in his church. It gave me more of a sense of God being present."

will require you to have someone in their altar guild make the sanctuary arrangement using the flowers or colors of your choosing. Sometimes they will ask you to donate that floral arrangement to the church following your wedding so that it may be used at the community's worship service. (Read more about flowers later.)

When the architecture of the church is strong and clean, frilly and ornate decorations detract from its integrity. Rarely is there reason, for example, to roll out a white runner for the procession, unless you will be sweeping in a long train down the center of a dusty, medieval cathedral. Filling the sanctuary with huge sprays of flowers or with brightly colored ribbons is, likewise, unnecessary and out of keeping with a church's overall structure.

The person who presides at the ceremony may suggest an arrangement of the sanctuary furniture that allows the central action of your wedding—the exchange of vows—to receive appropriate focus and to be seen by the assembly. It is inappropriate, however, to move the furnishings about on your own.

IT REALLY IRKS ME no end when some wedding coordinator comes in during the rehearsal wanting to move the altar and the pulpit and telling me where I can stand or not stand. This is a church, a liturgical space, and each piece has meaning. We're not putting on a school play.

Creating a Sacred Space Outside a Church

There are often reasons for choosing to marry in a setting other than a church—in a family member's home or garden, in a hotel banquet hall, or in nature. You may be from completely different religious traditions, for example, and find yourselves uncomfortable in either tradition's place of worship. Or you may have no feelings at all—or even negative ones—for a church. In such cases, you may want to consider other sites.

If you plan your wedding to take place somewhere other than a church, you will need to give more thought and energy to making it a holy space capable of "containing" your ceremony.

I'M A PRESBYTERIAN. Not a very good one, mind you, but I'm not giving up on it. My fiancé is Jewish and although he wouldn't have minded getting married in a church, his parents would have been upset. When they heard us discussing the possibility, they said if we married in a church, they felt they would not be able to attend. They seemed much easier with a compromise—so we settled on this lovely 1920s mission-style house that's rented out for weddings and other celebrations.

AFTER FOUR YEARS of living together and never bringing it up, we get engaged and suddenly my fiancée and I discover ourselves talking about religion! It's the business of how to get married when neither of us have stepped into a church since we were kids. There's something about "going to the altar," something about the size of the commitment we're making, something about our parents' expectations—and we don't want to hurt them—that makes us talk about religion. Even talking about raising kids in some kind of faith, but we don't know about that yet. Right now it looks like we'd just feel hypocritical having this church thing. But we would like a minister and we would like readings from the Bible. So Mom knows this minister we're going to talk to. If he's willing to do this for us in my parents' country club, I think that's the way we'll go. But in a church? I don't think so.

You look for a nice site perhaps, but there are three things you want the place to do.

First, you want it to hold a sense of the holy. In traditional Christian spirituality, beauty is an attribute of the divine. Some places are filled with so much natural beauty that there is nothing you could add to improve it. Other places, however, like hotel ballrooms, some halls, or backyards seem to have nothing sacred about them at all. You may need to create a sense of the sacred by what you bring to the place, something with quality and beauty. A table, a book stand, a hand-woven cloth, an Oriental rug, a cluster of candles, pots of flowers and ferns.

Second, you want the space to gather your guests into a community. Too often outdoor places—especially vast spaces—lack any sense of "containment." People feel lost or dwarfed because the space is too open and undefined. Then mark off a space—symbolically, if not literally—so that people know where to gather. You want your space to hold everyone in a fairly tight group, not thinly scattered. If at all possible, you want people gathered around you. Sometimes a circle of potted plants, or flags, banners, or wind socks will help create this space within a space.

And finally, you want the space to focus the community's attention on the central action. Paradoxically, what gives a place its palpable sense of the sacred may be the very thing that works against it as a place for a wedding ceremony. When surrounded by majestic mountains, for example, your guests may have a hard time paying attention to what the two of you are doing. It takes extra skill to gather and focus people in such a setting.

When we wish to make safe and bless the action we perform, we bless the space around it. We encircle it to contain something of the uncontainable. We mark the place and the time. We set it apart and prepare it for the visitation and the sanction of the Spirit.

We use the church, the house of the people of God. Or, without a church we create a space or a container, well circumscribed but "open at the top." By "open at the top" we mean to say that humankind can be contained and held, but not so the Spirit. The Spirit must be free to come and go. If our plans, our program, our time, or our space is overcontrolled or airtight or "fool-proof," it will also be "Spirit proof." Leave space for what is unplanned. Leave time where silence may speak. Leave some things undone and open to mystery. Expect the unexpected.

A COUPLE IN COLORADO planned their wedding for early September, hoping the aspen would be at their brightest gold. They reserved a room in a hotel with a view to the mountains and a vast aspen grove. The day of the wedding was magnificent, crystal-clear, and frosty. The aspen were, in fact, at the peak of their glory. The guests, fifty or so, milled around in the room visiting and admiring the view.

Then the minister asked everyone to gather around him and the couple at the far end of the room by a huge stone fireplace. The space was effectively set apart from the rest of the room by little more than the Oriental carpet on the floor. The minister commented on the beauty of their surroundings and then said, "But we are gathered to witness something even more beautiful, the promise of love and a lifelong commitment." He asked the people to bow their heads and he led them in a prayer. The bride's brother read a passage from Scripture, and the groom's cousin read a poem. The minister read a passage from the Gospels and then spoke about God's bounty, a bounty that showed itself both in nature and in love. Then he asked the guests to draw in even closer while the couple recited their vows. Everyone joined hands and prayed the Lord's Prayer together. They just stayed, clasping hands in what now was a circle around the couple and the minister. After the minister spoke the nuptial blessing over the couple, he said, "Our celebration has ended and yet has just begun. Please welcome the newlyweds as husband and wife!" The couple kissed. They kissed their parents. The people clapped and kissed each other and embraced the couple. Then they all walked back to the other part of the room, where the tables were set and champagne was being poured.

The People

Weddings involve people. Lots of people. Different people. Very different people. It falls to you, the bride and groom, to interact with all of them. There are musicians, caterers, bakers, photographers, printers, janitors, maybe calligraphers. Checklists and wedding planners will help you make your way through this confusion of people.

This chapter will highlight only those people who most directly affect your wedding ceremony. Your families, children if you have them, and close friends. Yourselves. The bridesmaids and groomsmen (whom we refer to as witnesses). Your guests. The presider. The wedding coordinator, if you choose one. And the photographers (who call for special consideration because they can be an ever-present shadow to your every action).

Family and Friends

Weddings bring out the best and the worst in people. You can expect some people to be bighearted, generous, and supportive while others may launch into crazy-making responses. When they are at their best, your relatives and friends will see every aspect of your wedding—from its preparations and social celebrations to the wedding day itself—as an occasion to demonstrate their love for you. Many will be exceptionally generous, volunteering to help with the finances or with your long lists of practical details. Some may overcome their reticence and, possibly for the first time, address past misunderstandings in order to make amends. Or some who were distant will reestablish and strengthen their love and friendship with you. In experiences like these, it is the Spirit at work, the Spirit who blesses and upholds you.

At their worst, people will hold grudges, make thoughtless comments, be passive-aggressive, competitive, unreliable, inflexible, controlling, or unwilling to compromise. Major celebrations, like a wedding, magnify a family's pet dysfunctions. There are those who will be sullen and noncommunicative, refusing to talk to certain people or to attend any event where "those people" are present. Some will be subtly negative, while others will be dramatic. Some will insist that their desires and values take precedence over yours, laying down conditions and terrorizing everyone. They will dredge up long-forgotten hurts that will cause other people pain and turmoil. Those who abuse alcohol or drugs may increase their usage and their destructive behavior. In general, they can make

MY SISTER came out from Nebraska to help me with the wedding. I hadn't spent time with her in ages. We stayed up into the wee hours one night just talking. There was so much to work out between us. As kids we were close—we were only nineteen months apart. Oh, scrappy, too, you know, competitive. But when she married and moved to Nebraska and I went east we entered our own worlds. In the course of our conversation that night we discovered that some of our petty competition wasn't resolved. Stuff you'd think we would have outgrown was still sitting between us—like did Mom think my sister was prettier than me and love sewing for her and was Dad prouder of me because I was the brainy bookworm. You know, my sister's learned a lot by having two daughters of her own. She brought a lot of wisdom to our conversation that I didn't know she had. Anyhow, by the time we finished talking, it felt so good! Like I got my sister back again.

THIS WAS MY SECOND MARRIAGE and I knew it had to be different—everything about it had to be more grown-up—adult—than when I first married. So first I put on my own bachelor party with all the guys from my department and I also invited my dad! We had a sit-down dinner and every guy had to stand up and give his most valued piece of wisdom about marriage or life. The guys ranged in age from twenty-seven to my dad, who was seventy-eight. Now, I knew my father loved me, but he wasn't the kind to get all emotional. At the bachelor dinner he got up and said, "Here's my wisdom. It's always important to admit your mistakes. Ask for forgiveness and state your affections." (I liked that, "State your affections.") Then he went on. "I made the mistake of never telling my son straight out how much I love him and how proud I am of him. I thought that wasn't manly. I was wrong. And I'm sorry. He and his brother are the greatest gift his mother and I ever had. I'm sorry I didn't tell him this earlier, but I'm gonna tell him now in front of all these young men, Son, I love you. Very much." Well, there followed a bit of nose blowing. I can tell you that every guy there probably wished he'd been their dad too.

your wedding as difficult as possible for you and your guests. These are the threshold spirits at work.

When people bless you with their affection, there is little you have to do. Open yourselves to the Spirit and be grateful and glad. Even if you feel embarrassed by their generosity, accept it with grace and say thank you.

When besieged by the spirits of discord and destruction, draw the peace of the Spirit around yourselves. Do whatever protects you. While you can't change other people or their craziness at this point, you can support each other. Resist being caught in other people's struggles and power games. Resolve from the start not to let yourselves be divided.

MY PARENTS TOLD ME, politely but firmly, that they wouldn't attend my wedding, since I was marrying a divorced woman and they morally disapproved of this marriage.

RIGHT BEFORE THE WEDDING BEGAN, just as I was getting ready to start the procession, my sister snipped: "It really frosts me, the way your wedding is upstaging mine. You always have to one-up me."

LISTEN! You will *not* believe this one. My friend, the mother of the bride, had gone through an ugly divorce and hadn't talked to her ex for years. At the wedding she was escorted to the front pew. Then the new wife was escorted down the aisle. She insisted on being seated in the front pew! She just stood there in front of everyone and told the mother of the bride to move back to the second pew so she could sit up front next to the bride's father, her husband.

Remind yourselves of a few simple truths.

Other people's negativity has less to say about the two of you and more to say about them. Make a concerted effort not to take hurtful comments personally or be affected by what other people do. Protect yourselves from what goes on around you by constantly supporting each other and reminding each other that other people's problems are precisely that: their problems.

Readjust your expectations. You can't expect yourselves to be perfectly cool, perfectly loving, and perfectly mature throughout everything leading up to your wedding. You can't expect other people to be perfect either. All of us are human and have our little quirks to contribute to the mix. When you are the ones who make mistakes or cause other people pain, apologize and ask for forgiveness. By doing so you will set the tone for those around you.

Remember that the two of you share a deep love. The certainty of your love makes you strong, and because of it you are wiser and more at peace than all those who, in their confusion, scatter contention and discord. Between you, you have so much love that you can afford to spread it around. Give it away. Like yeast, love multiplies, it doesn't divide. Touch every situation with your love, your calm, and your reassurance, and you will leave even the most difficult people feeling blessed. Be as gentle

---

He drew a circle that shut me out—

Heretic, rebel, a thing to flout.

But Love and I had the wit to win—

We drew a circle that took him in!

as you can with those friends and relatives who, for whatever reason, flail around and cause disorder. When the going gets tough, pray for increased generosity and inclusivity.

And finally, pray together for wisdom and peace. Pray with gratitude for your mutual love. Pray for everyone you are gathering to witness your love and for those who have even minor parts to play in making this wedding day come together. Ask God's blessings on them. The simple prayer of St. Francis of Assisi covers a multitude of situations:

Lord, make me an instrument of your peace.
Where there is hatred, let me sow love.
Where there is injury, pardon.
Where there is discord, unity.
Where there is doubt, faith.
Where there is error, truth.
Where there is despair, hope.
Where there is sadness, joy.
Where there is darkness, light.
O Divine Master, grant that I may not so much seek
To be consoled, as to console,
To be understood, as to understand,
To be loved, as to love.
For it is in giving that we receive,
It is in pardoning that we are pardoned,
And it is in dying that we are born to eternal life.

The Two of You

You are the central symbols of the wedding. And yet, paradoxi-cally, precisely because you are the focus, it is important that you resist every temptation to draw further attention to yourselves. Everyone has already naturally turned your way at this time, and you need do nothing further to demand attention. Since the rit-uals of a wedding—the social events as well as the ceremony—establish your dignity and importance, don't complicate matters by piling on additional demands for personal attention. Strip away what is superfluous—overly lavish attire, monumental flower arrangements, the chauffeur-driven limousine. You already stand at the center. Take your place with dignity and grace.

NOW YOU CAN WORK on becoming nobody, which is really somebody. For when you become nobody there is no tension, no pretense, no one trying to be anyone or anything. The natural state of the mind shines through unobstructed—and the natural state of the mind is pure love.

—Ram Dass

The vows you exchange are the central action of the wedding. They are a bold, almost reckless act of selfless love, and they set the standard by which every other word, gesture, and action of your celebration will be understood. The love you pledge to each other overflows and spreads out to everyone who has gath-ered by your side. The quality of the love and respect you share determines the value of your wedding, not the financial excess you lavish on it.

As the host and hostess of the celebration, blessed by the presence of your guests, be graciously attentive to their comfort and enjoyment.

Plan the wedding so that it is a mutual reflection of your personalities and values.

Talk to each other about the celebrations you remember, especially about the religious ceremonies that touched you. Reflect together about what made them special. Discuss your ethnic backgrounds and the family traditions that were a part of your growing up. Brainstorm. Get a huge sheet of paper and write it all down. From all these considerations a style will emerge that will satisfy both of you. Any wedding that ends up looking just like someone else's or imitates one you read about or saw promoted at a wedding fair—beautiful as it may be—won't be *your* wedding.

There is, however, a distinction between suiting the wedding to your style and styling your wedding to very personal or private tastes. Just because you met in a hot air balloon, for example, is no reason to marry in a balloon. But if you are more comfortable at square dances than at black tie affairs, you will be happier planning an informal wedding and reception.

WE MADE A concerted effort to protect ourselves from the wiles of the commercial wedding world by dealing first with what was truly important to *both* of us. Together and with my mom and his mom, we wrote on cards all the issues that came to mind. Then we took the pile and laid the cards out across the floor in order of importance. Right off, we came up with two names of ministers in the family who could do our ceremony. Attire, flowers, decorations at the reception . . . these came way down the line to be dictated by place, budget, and style. Our moms suggested we take some of these details and pass them out to friends or family. A favorite aunt and uncle had the perfect house for the reception. Another aunt was wonderful with flowers and was delighted to make simple boutonnieres, bouquets, and arrangements for the wedding as her gift to us. My grandmother was thrilled to sew my dress for me. My mother-in-law baked a special wedding cake from a recipe that was in that family for years. Everybody said it was the best and most unusual wedding cake they'd ever tasted. We had more fun planning together and we loved involving both families.

A MAN WHO LOVES his woman and is enthusiastic about their marriage isn't necessarily gung-ho about the big-deal wedding. I think he just stands around and lets her do whatever she wants—if that's what makes her happy—let her. If all this is necessary to start the marriage for her, well, okay. But I think a lot of men would be perfectly happy to have a small, solid ceremony followed by a good party.

WELL, WOMEN'S LIBERATION still hasn't shown up too much in how weddings get planned, I don't think. For all their talk about equality, it's still the woman who plans the wedding around herself and keeps the man in a position of minimal involvement.

WE COULDN'T DO one of those "traditional weddings" where the bride and her folks do all the work, make all the decisions, and pay all the bills. Those days are over. After consulting our parents, we made most of the decisions ourselves. We split the costs between us and our parents on both sides made contributions to the wedding kitty. That felt really good.

The Guests

A wedding wouldn't be a wedding without at least a few people in attendance. Although your vows are the central action of the wedding, what makes it a wedding is the fact that others witness your vows. Your guests are more than passive observers; they are witnesses. They surround you with their loving support and, in effect, say "amen" to your vows.

Whether you invite only two people to stand by you or hundreds of family members and friends, the more you involve your guests in the occasion, the richer and more satisfying your celebration will be. In other times and places, the entire community marked a couple's wedding, each person having a part to play. Today, however, we are less likely to live in a close-knit community. And our modern experience has conditioned us to be passive, to be entertained, to be inclined more to watch than to take part in the action. For that reason it will take greater effort to involve your guests in your wedding.

When the Roman Catholic church revised its worship and rituals in the 1960s, one of its guiding principles was the "full and active participation" of each person. Adopt the same guideline. Ask yourselves how you can involve your guests as fully and as actively in your wedding as possible. Some can serve as greeters, ushers, readers, and altar servers. Others can offer special prayers. All of them can sing or pray or extend a blessing over you.

The decision to involve your guests in the wedding has many repercussions. You may decide, for example, to print up a small pamphlet that outlines the order of worship and allows people unfamiliar with the structure of the service to follow it. (See the section on the order of worship.) Or you can select songs that most people will be able to sing. You can pose for photographs before the ceremony instead of after it, so as not to keep your guests waiting at the reception.

The Guest List

Make your guest list by first inviting those friends and relatives you most want to celebrate with you, those who will support you in the years to come.

While you will want to be generous in drawing up your list, your budget will restrict you. You can afford to pay for only so many guests at your reception. If your parents are helping with expenses, they will expect to invite certain family members and friends of their own. They may also want to invite business associates. As your list swells, you have to make some difficult decisions. If your parents' values clash with your own, they will do so most dramatically over the question of who is and is not invited. "Drawing the line" is one of the more painful aspects of planning your wedding.

Even the most tightly drawn list should include the people you love most. If you can't afford to invite them, reconsider your reception plans. You may have to choose between a lavish reception with fewer of the people you love in attendance and a modest reception with more friends present.

The guest list will usher you into an area inhabited by the most irritable and pesky ghosts. Relatives and friends who have been absent from your life for quite some time may suddenly appear. They will feel entitled to an invitation and be hurt when they are "excluded." At the same time, some people will secretly resent being invited, thinking you asked them to attend only so they would be obliged to give you a gift.

Reconcile yourselves to the fact that you can't please everyone. Tapping into the deep love you have for each other will give you the strength and wisdom you need. Support each other to deflect other people's negativity and respond maturely to those who act inappropriately. This is one of those moments when your love and solidarity can serve as a model of healing for those who are agitated or hurting on the sidelines.

Choosing Witnesses

Weddings and state laws require only two witnesses. Rather than have an unwieldy retinue of men and women in attendance, many couples simply ask the two most important people in their

---

AN OLDER COUPLE, both widowed and active in the cathedral, married in a formal ceremony. The procession was led by his two grandsons; one carried incense and the other carried the processional cross. The bride's best friend walked behind, carrying the lectionary, the book of readings. The priest followed her with two altar servers, the son and daughter of the couple's mutual friends. The groom, accompanied by his adult children and their families, walked in next. The woman followed. Her two granddaughters carrying candles preceded her. Her sons and their wives surrounded her. When the appropriate time came, two friends stepped forward to serve as witnesses and others helped distribute communion. Everyone felt involved in the wedding, and no one noticed the lack of attendants.

---

lives to be their witnesses. Some couples choose witnesses without regard to their gender. A groom may choose his sister to be his witness or a bride her brother. Additional attendants, even for a formal wedding, are unnecessary.

Close friends and other members of your families will still feel part of your wedding even if they aren't your witnesses as long as you involve them some other way. Invite them to greet the guests at the door and to seat them. Give them a reading to proclaim. Ask them to join the company that takes you down the aisle in the entry procession.

When you ask people to be your witnesses, you honor them for their affection and for the roles they play in your lives. It is a burden as well as an honor, since it costs them in time, money, and perhaps travel. Their expenses are a gift to you.

Children from a Previous Marriage

If either of you has children, you will want to involve them in your wedding with sensitivity. If they are adults, you can simply tell them you'd like them to participate and ask them how they feel about it. You may have to listen patiently and respectfully as they sort through their mixed feelings or unfinished business. Depending on their responses, they might join the procession with you, serve as your witnesses, proclaim a reading, or offer one of the prayers.

Teenagers are more likely to have conflicting feelings—some of which have little to do with your remarriage—and may lack the ability to articulate their feelings. Be sensitive to what they say and, more important, to what they don't say. Help them find the words to express themselves. In your own words, mirror back to them whatever they share, and check to see if you understand them perfectly. By letting them know that you hear and understand them, you are helping them more than you think.

Younger children also call for delicacy, tact, and wisdom on your part. Depending on their ages and level of development, they may be more or less in touch with their feelings. Maybe they like the person you are marrying. Maybe they don't. They may feel torn between their love for you and their loyalty to their other parent. Perhaps they still secretly hope that you and their other parent will get back together again, and, if so, they may feel compelled to resist your current plans. If they haven't had the chance to work through their feelings about your divorce, they may be emotionally overwhelmed by a wedding. If you and your former spouse are committed to your children's welfare, the two of you may be able to help them deal with their feelings. Or you might ask another person—a grandparent, an aunt, a teacher—to talk to your children for you.

Above all, you want your children—no matter what their ages—to know that you love them and want them to be a part of your festivities in a way that respects them and respects their feelings.

The Presider

Your plans and choices—your personalities alone—will not make the sacred rites of your wedding just happen. You will need to seek out a leader, someone with the vision, experience, and authority to help make your ceremony come alive. Someone who will lead you into the sacred moment and through it. Someone who will invoke God's blessing on you and your promises to each other.

In most Christian churches the traditional leader for a wedding is the minister, priest, deacon, or elder. They are the community's leaders, the people who both serve and represent the community. They have a special role in the community's worship, but they don't act alone. They don't "do" the community's worship, they lead the community as it worships. And they don't "do" weddings, they witness the marriages of people who are members of their community. Throughout this book we will refer to them as "presiders," the ones who lead the community in celebrating your wedding.

Remember, when you look for a church and a priest or minister for your wedding, a church isn't a hall like any other hall you might rent for a wedding, and a priest or minister isn't a "vendor" of services like a florist or photographer.

Good presiders are sensitive to the holiness of marriage, familiar with the ebb and flow of a sacred ritual, and committed to setting a dignified tone. They spend time getting to know you, preparing you for marriage, planning your ceremony, and praying with you. They consider what they are doing to be a ministry, a service performed in faith. Although they may request a donation for their time and for the church, they aren't hired help, and it is discourteous to order them around.

If you are connected with a church, you may ask the priest or minister there to perform your ceremony. Or if you know someone personally—a relative or a family friend who is a clergyperson—you may ask him or her to be your presider. If you have no church affiliation, you may have more difficulty locating a presider. Begin a search by asking your friends who have recently been married.

MY FORMER WIFE is getting married again. The guy's a good fellow. I'm pleased for her. It's our son we're concerned about. We've been talking together about how we can help him. We knew it was going to be tough on him, and sure enough he's gotten clingy and whiny. I've gone out of my way to spend time with him and to tell him how much I love him. I tell him even though Mommy is going to have a new husband, I will always be his daddy.

WHEN MY DAUGHTER REMARRIED, she did something that made me very uneasy. Understandably, she wanted her son, our ten-year-old grandson, to take part in her wedding. He processed in with us—we were all surrounding her—which was fine. That was a nice touch, actually. Her fiancé also walked in with his mother and stepfather. But then she had her son come up and be part of the exchange of vows! She had that poor kid and her fiancé essentially vow to be father and son! I know she did it because she wanted the boy to feel part of things. But I also think she did it to make herself feel better. This was a really painful thing for the boy—and confusing! He did it, but he also felt like he was disowning his own dad.

ARE THEY REALLY DOING THINGS like that in second marriages with children? I was at a wedding recently, where the groom gave a ring to his bride and then he gave little rings to each of his two daughters. Whose wedding is this? I happen to know that the girls, in this case, have been having a very hard time adjusting to the remarriage and had felt left out during the courtship. Something like that just makes me think: Don't jerk your *kids* around so that *you* feel better!

If you choose to marry in a nonreligious setting, you can still find a presider. There are ministers who specialize in performing weddings. You can find them, if all else fails, in the phone book or in the wedding section that appears weekly in most newspapers. Many also advertise their services on the Internet.

If you use the services of a judge or a justice of the peace, you will likely need to give much more thought and attention to how you can honor the spiritual aspect of your marriage.

Wedding Coordinator

Wedding coordinators can be helpful in arranging the details of a wedding's social gatherings, most especially the reception. They orchestrate the behind-the-scenes elements of hospitality so you can be free to enjoy yourselves and be fully present for the more important issues. Coordinators who have been trained in the dynamics of a sacred ritual can help you at the ceremony. They can make sure, for example, that everyone is in position for the entrance procession. Wedding coordinators unfamiliar with a religious celebration, however, may be unable to provide the help you are looking for. Decide before you interview coordinators what you want of them.

A growing number of churches have a person or a group of people trained to help coordinate the service itself. They work with you during the rehearsal and the ceremony and take care of the last-minute details that will otherwise overwhelm you.

Photographers/Videographers

There's a cartoon of a family on vacation. They have pulled over to a scenic viewpoint, snapped photographs, and are rushing back to their car. A child protests, wanting to linger over the view and the father barks, "We don't have time for that now. You can look at the pictures when we get home."

A wedding is, above all, a living event, meant to be experienced in the moment as fully and as directly as possible by everyone present. Photographs are a fine reminder of the event, but they are not the event itself. Too often photographers intrude into the scene, not always to record it but to stage it, stopping the flow of the celebration. When you interview potential photographers, look for one who has the talent to capture moments unobtrusively, and as they happen.

If you want posed photographs, meet with your photographer and the wedding party *before* the ceremony. Doing so cuts down on the time your guests have to wait for you at the reception.

Having someone videotape your wedding often causes more trouble than it is worth: Some video cameras require bright lights that spoil the atmosphere of the wedding, and videographers tend to be even more obtrusive than regular photographers.

Be sure your photographer speaks to the presider before the ceremony begins so they can agree about the use of flash photography and about when and where photographs may be taken. Many churches have explicit written directives that you can give the photographer beforehand.

People. All kinds of people will be part of your wedding. And

I PERFORMED a wedding for a couple from overseas. Since most of their family members were unable to attend the ceremony, they hired a photographer and two videographers. I spoke with them before the ceremony and told them precisely where they were allowed to stand. I asked them not to use flash photography and not to use floodlights on their video cameras. When it came time for the vows, however, they closed right in. They became so obtrusive, I'm sure no one in the congregation saw the couple exchange their vows. One of them actually scrambled *over the tops* of three pews to position himself favorably. It took everything in me not to bring the ceremony to a halt and stare the man down.

THE WEDDING TOOK PLACE in Sweden on an island. The bride grew all the flowers herself. Her mother and aunties prepared the food. Her sisters baked the three-tiered fruit torte. Her family's summer house where the reception would be held was walking distance from the island's white wooden church. The sea sparkled. The American guests were dazzled. The Swedish family was warm and hospitable. Everyone filed into the little church where the woodwork was painted its traditional dusty blue and the sun played off the white walls. Everybody sang their heads off. The groom lost his cool and wept freely. Everybody followed suit. What happened was, the kindly minister gave us the occasion and the freedom to be fully present. He smiled at us before the procession began and said, "No photography, please. I will let you know when you can bring out your cameras." At the end of the service, he turned the beaming couple to the people and presented them to us as husband and wife. "Now you may photograph!" he added. And of course, the snapshots were wonderful. There was exuberance in the air. There were only beaming smiling faces. In fact, we pooled all the snapshots and made them a wedding book. They didn't even need those posed pictures we agonize over in "our tradition."

these months of planning and moving among every sort of personality type will test your love and kindness. Make this prayer your breathing mantra for the days ahead:

> *May I,*
> *together with all beings,*
> *enjoy a refreshed sense*
> *of kindness in mind,*
> *joyfulness of heart,*
> *and an expansiveness of being.*

Sacred Symbols

A wedding ceremony is carefully composed of words, actions, music, rituals, and symbols. Together they serve to give depth and power to this sacred occasion.

A good symbol has a power all its own and appeals to the whole person, our feeling, doing, and thinking. Even if we can't quite put words to our feeling, a symbol lets us know in our very bones that something profound is happening. Remember how you felt when you craned your neck to watch your friend's baby being baptized? When you received flowers from this person you so love? When you watched a casket being lowered into a grave and you helped cover it with earth? You know the power of symbol.

I TOOK A CLASS as part of my preparation to become a deacon. The professor talked of sacramental signs and symbols. He said a symbol has the power to touch us far beyond our understanding. But there was this guy in the class who kept arguing with him. He said a thing is just a thing. That's all. Nothing more. One day the professor said to him casually, "I see you are wearing a ring. What's it worth to you?" The guy didn't answer. "I'll tell you what," the professor went on. "We'll have it appraised and I'll buy it from you for its full value." The guy acted confused and said the professor must be crazy. This was his wedding ring! Money couldn't buy what it meant to him. "Precisely what I've been saying," the professor replied. "I rest my case."

Symbols speak for themselves. They need no embellishment. When we don't trust that others will "get it," we explain what the symbol means or, worse, we layer it with additional actions, words, or emphasis. Exchanging rings, like shaking hands or giving a kiss, needs no explanation, no amplification.

When symbols fail to catch hold of us, it may be for one of two reasons. Perhaps the symbol is not authentic. It may have been cut away from its archetypal roots and become merely arcane. It may be a relic that has lost its power and no longer speaks to a new time and culture. It may have been recently invented and contrived. Symbols that have grown thin and anemic may be better discarded than explained.

Other symbols, however, may be weak and ineffective because they are presented in a stingy and pinched manner. Or the gestures are not generous and thoughtful. A sacred sign reduced to an anemic pro forma gesture needs to be fully and generously restored. Explanations—more words—will do nothing to save it;

the symbol must be returned to its innate archetypal value. Then the symbol and the action will reach into the deep places of the soul and quicken anyone who stands there as witness.

In this chapter we address the difference between personal symbols, symbols from an ethnic heritage, and the symbols that are the most important symbols in a wedding, the authentic ones that belong to all of us. They include the two of you as the central symbol, the rings, the vows, special attire, the altar or table, the cross, the book, the kiss, candles, incense, food, water, and flowers. We suggest ways of giving them due reverence, freeing them from unnecessary clutter and restoring their true worth.

As you plan the ceremony, you will consider each symbol, turning it over in your mind and imagination and reflecting on it. What does this mean? Not just to the two of you privately but for the whole assembly gathered around you? What does it say? What feeling does it evoke in us? How is this best presented? Is this something we need to reclaim, reframe, or throw out?

THE PRIEST BAPTIZED the baby with a thin squirt of water. He just reached into a box that was supposed to be a font—a pool of living water—and took out this little plastic squeeze bottle with green stuff growing in the bottom of it. He squirted a dribble on the child's hair. The symbol of baptism—of washing with living waters, of drowning and rising again, of being reborn—was reduced to a meaningless trickle. Just enough to fulfill a rule and obligation. The experience of that baptism may have been "valid," but it didn't move anyone. The water needed to be fresh and abundant, the gestures generous. Everyone was entitled to see it and hear it. The baby should have gotten wet. . . .

Personal Symbols

Personal symbols, those that come from our individual experiences and memories, lack the universal appeal of symbols that arise from our collective heritage. Personal symbols may mean something privately, but often mean little or nothing to the gathered group. Instead of trying to make your private symbol mean something to others, work it into the festivities in a subtle way. Best to let it have its place in the social events surrounding the ceremony.

THEY RAISED DOGS. Huskies. This was their life! I knew they'd get a husky into that wedding one way or another. So they used an image of two huskies in the wedding invitation. It was discreet—it was all right. Very subtle. But then I heard the bride was considering having their dog, Moluk, actually be the ring bearer. Gratefully, the minister talked them out of it. He was very wise. Without putting them down or being condescending, he brought them around to nixing it on their own. The bride told me about it and admitted that now she could see it could have been tacky.

Family/Social Symbols

All of us come from an ethnic or national heritage, however far back it may be. Our families may have handed on to us ethnic or national customs reaching back several generations. Cultural observances and symbols connected with our childhood and family of origin arouse memories, bring the past into the present, join

WHEN OUR SON MARRIED, my husband and I brought an old tradition into the reception party—something we did at our own wedding in Austria and had photos of. We made a log crib—a holder for a log—and we set a log in it. Then we decorated the crib and a big, long two-handed saw with flowers, and the newlyweds had to saw the log in half, learning how to work together equally and cooperate in the action of sawing in unison. It looked really pretty in its setting and everyone got into it, cheering them on and kidding them. They did it though! Determined to show us they knew how to work together.

one generation to another. They offer a timeless moment when the indestructible parts of self and tradition meet.

Does your family's cultural heritage have traditional symbols or customs that can be tastefully brought into the ceremony, or, better, integrated into the reception?

The "something borrowed" we speak of in a wedding may put you quietly in touch with your family heritage.

Those who have no strong religious convictions or a connection to an ethnic or cultural heritage of their own are sometimes tempted to adopt symbols or traditions from another culture. While you might feel you are honoring the culture in question by using its tradition, the true holders of these customs and practices often consider such "borrowing" a form of cultural piracy. They feel it is disrespectful to usurp what is freighted with meaning, possibly part of their secret rites, sacred, ancient, and an important aspect of their identity. Furthermore, it rarely ever works. Outside of its own context, it loses authenticity and comes off as contrived.

BY THE TIME we were to be married, both of us had just lost grandparents we loved and were close to. We were really sad that they weren't going to be at our wedding. So we decided to use a beautiful rug and a runner from both their houses at the wedding. One we laid out approaching the altar and the other one we stood on during the ceremony. We felt like they were our foundation and heritage right there under us. Seeing those rugs out of their usual context brought up some fantastic stories and memories from other family members.

The Central Symbol: The Couple

The two of you, as the marrying partners, stand at the center of the wedding ceremony. Bride and groom are the most important symbol. You represent the archetype of wholeness—the coming together of all opposites into unity and balance—a mythical marriage of heaven and earth. For this moment, time stops and everything is perfection: perfect balance, perfect cooperation, perfect harmony, perfect unity. When Jesus talked about if-this-were-a-perfect-world (what he called the "reign of God"), he told parables of a wedding feast. In a wedding, every good thing comes together and is made a new and holy entity.

Since the coming together of bride and groom represents wholeness and balance, you can easily see how well balanced the ritual gestures of a wedding need to be. The roles of bride and groom, while separate, require equal intensity of value. Any inequity between them can't communicate harmony or balance.

In our time, we are trying hard to return equal value to the genders, and, hence, equal value to their roles in a wedding ceremony.

I'VE BEEN MARRIED for twenty-eight years now and my son will surely be marrying soon himself. I have strong feelings about the role I wanted for myself when I married and about the kind of role I hope he can wrest in these times. What is often in short supply at weddings is a complete, three-dimensional role for the man. This speaks about an unconscious recognition that very often marriage is less significant for the man than for the woman—and that is a damned shame. Yes, in a traditional wedding the man does things. He says things first, lifts the veil, kisses the bride, and leads her down the aisle to the exit. He participates, but is he involved? What could bring him more into the whole process? Who decided that this marriage is less significant to him?

WITH ALL THE EMPHASIS on me as the bride—the pressure to make so many decisions, to be so unremittingly center stage—everyone else involved in the festivities—including the groom!—seriously has to take care not to "upstage" me. What a commentary! So much for the equality of the sexes. And so much for the centrality of the vows we will exchange. There's no way I can do it that so-called "traditional way." No way!

When all the costs and work, emphasis, drama, and action center around one partner, we have to wonder what we're saying about marriage. Is this a reaction against other inequities? Is it a concept promoted by the commercial world which profits from all the cultural expectations placed on the bride to make it her day? To reclaim your true value as a symbol of wholeness and balance, the two of you need to be equally involved and represented in the wedding. Neither one should require more of the spotlight than the other. Neither one should be required to fade into the wings.

When you turn and speak your vows to each other, your words have a power that reaches out far beyond yourselves. Like rain in a desert, those words fall on thirsty ground. They revitalize the commitments of all those present who have made the same vows to each other before. Your vows renew their vows. Speak them loudly so everyone hears.

Everyone is moved to do his and her own part in bringing a right balance and harmony into the world with love and mutual respect and empathy.

You are the ones that both the presider and the people now bless. In this moment, the two of you become holy to each other and offer each other yourselves in total commitment.

For Christians, the couple is also a symbol of God's love for humankind, a symbol of the marriage of the divine to the human. Out of love for us, God took flesh in Jesus to live with us. The Incarnation means literally taking on flesh. God took on everything there is about being human, even the flesh of our bodies with its sexuality. A couple's sexual life—their ability to unite with each other in mutual self-giving and joy and to bring forth life—is a sign of and a participation in God's creativity.

One of the greatest mysteries of the Christian faith—the Incarnation—is expressed through what is utterly natural. By sharing our flesh, God allows us a hand in creating and bringing about a more perfect world. In marriage we confer that sacred mystery on each other and know what balance it takes for husband and wife to become one in mind and heart and body. In marriage—in essence, in the joining of every split in opposites, as much as in the mystery of the incarnation—masculine and feminine, earth and heaven, body and Spirit are united and equally important in the creation of the new and the holy.

The Rings

Wedding rings are powerful symbols. Like every circle, they speak of continuity, eternity, wholeness, completion. As a symbol of marriage they remind you of the seasons of your love, the recurring time-cycles you share with each other. They also remind you—and others—of your identity. You are someone's wife. You are someone's husband. And not because you own each other, but because the love you pledge each other is freely committed and eternal.

You have chosen your rings, perhaps even designed them, with a great deal of thought. But, in essence, they need be nothing more than a band of gold—a most precious metal. Throughout history, gold has denoted highest value, consciousness, and immutability. Purified by fire, gold does not rust, corrode, or tarnish. It increases the value of even the simplest object. Early alchemists believed that gold was spun sunlight that came from the eternal orbiting of earth and sun. As spun sunlight, gold illumines your marriage with divine insight and courage.

In most Christian ceremonies, before the bride and groom present them to each other, the presider blesses the wedding rings. In some traditions, the presider sprinkles them with holy water as part of the blessing, and by doing so recalls the couple's baptisms and explicitly links their married life to their Christian life.

Throughout the centuries, people have worn wedding rings on various fingers. In our day the fourth finger of the left hand has become the ring finger, because an early anatomist believed it had a direct line of contact to the heart.

Since rings have rich value and symbolic power, why would

WHEN WE MARRY, I will give my fiancé the gold band my great-grandfather wore. When I asked his permission, he was thrilled! He said it made him feel like he was a part of a historical line. We're going to take it to a jeweler to have it polished and to have the date of our wedding engraved inside, next to the date of my great-grandparents' wedding.

MY GRANDFATHER told me that when he and Grandmother married, you put the wedding ring partway down the thumb and said, "In the name of the Father," then you put it over the index finger and said, "and of the Son," and then you put it on the middle finger and said: "and of the Holy Ghost." Then you put it on the ring finger and said: "Amen." My other grandparents, who are from Germany, wore their wedding bands on their left hands during their engagement period and at their wedding switched them to their right hands. That's the way it was done there.

WE WERE MARRIED at my family home. On the morning of the wedding, the families were all there, milling around, having a wonderful, lively brunch. It was mayhem. Even if it was happy stuff, it was mayhem! I realize now that we would have gone rather clumsily from that brunch into the wedding ceremony if that nice priest hadn't had the greatest idea! With plenty of time before all the guests arrived, he gathered the two families together in the garden in a close circle with us in the middle. Then he brought out our rings. He had laid them in a nice dish, and he had my dad's ice bucket with water in it. He blessed the water, asking it to do all sorts of special things for us, and then he gave every person present the chance to come up and bless our rings with the water and say a blessing for us and for our marriage. Everybody had time to think about what they might say and came up when they felt ready—and, brother, there wasn't a dry eye in the crowd. We heard things and felt things that never would have been delivered or received without that quiet ceremony. We moved from there into the wedding itself completely transformed and transfixed. We were *ready*. By the way, we just love that priest for what he did for us. We'll never forget it.

---

we give them to a child to bring forward in a procession? It makes even less sense to sew imitations on a lace pillow for the youngster to carry while the real rings are hidden in some adult's pocket. Children are certainly cute, but there is no symbolic reason for them to carry the rings. As they are launched from point A and pushed off in the direction of point B, everyone watches and wonders if they will make it down the aisle. Children may offer a moment of levity—but is it comic relief we need at the start of a sacred ceremony? Is it the job of a child to carry the rings of love and fidelity to two adults?

The Bride's Dress

Think "bride" and you promptly think: white dress and gossamer veils. The white wedding dress is a common Western or European tradition, though not a universal one. The Chinese bride, for instance, wears red, the color of rejoicing. Other cultures have outfits that come from their own traditions: crowns, flowered or ribboned wreaths, or wreaths of myrtle.

At one point in our tradition the white bridal dress signified bridal virginity. Not very long ago, brides who wore white made a public statement that is harder to make today. We have kept the dress but reframed its symbolism. It no longer signifies literal virginity, but has taken on the sense of new beginnings.

What most people don't know is that this white dress refers to another white garment Christians are familiar with: the baptismal gown or the baptismal garment. Some babies brought to the church for baptism wear a long white dress, often something that has been in the family for generations, or the presider may give them a white linen garment as a symbol of their new life in Christ. In some churches, adults who are baptized on the night of the Easter Vigil are given a white garment to wear. The presider says to infants and adults alike: You have become a new creation and have clothed yourself in Christ.

Vestiges of the baptismal garment can still be seen in the alb that some clergy wear during worship services, in the Easter outfit, and in the bride's gown. It can even be seen in the pall, the white cloth that is laid over the casket in a Christian funeral. All of these elements without exception speak of a fresh new beginning.

WHEN I WAS CONFIRMED, all of us were asked to bring something to the ceremony that we'd worn for our baptism and either tuck it into our pockets or wear it or something. We couldn't find a thing. And because I didn't have a baptismal robe, my mom made me a white stole for confirmation. When I married, she brought it out and asked me if I wanted to wear it for my wedding. It really seemed like a nice thing, but my husband didn't have a stole, and I thought he needed something even more than I did, because I had the white dress. Then his mom brought over the booties he'd worn when he was baptized and we took the ribbons out of them and incorporated them into a design for a stole for him. I made something for each of our children when they were baptized just keeping this in mind for their futures.

Giving the wedding dress the wrong kind of emphasis—making it too lavish, too dramatic, too expensive, too sexy, too girlish—reduces its symbolic significance and makes us forget that it is an outward sign of an inner truth. Brides will want to keep in mind the difference between a regal procession and a bride's entry into a new life.

The Veil

The bridal veil comes from a time when the bride's father literally gave her in marriage to the groom. In those days of arranged marriages, the groom often did not see the bride until their wedding day. Throughout the ceremony she was kept hidden behind a veil until, after the exchange of vows, the groom was allowed to lift the veil and take a look at this person he'd just married. And she in turn got a clearer vision of him. The unveiling was literally and figuratively a moment of revelation.

For couples who still hold to the custom, lifting the "fingertip veil," a short veil that covers the face, repeats an action left over from another time and culture even while it has become only a figurative "first revelation."

The veil, for reasons beyond explanation, remains part of our culture's bridal image. Some brides add a wreath of myrtle, orange blossoms, or fragrant herbs for their own symbolic and traditional value. (In second marriages, brides often omit the veil altogether, retaining only flowers or a wreath.) Who knows? Perhaps our culture has already reframed the meaning of the wedding veil: Marriage is veiled in mystery for which the loving work of self-revelation has only begun.

WHEN I MARRIED thirty-five years ago, I dressed at home, surrounded by my mother and my sisters, who helped me prepare. My father paced the floor downstairs and waited for us to descend in our combined and full glory. It may have taken him two trips in the family car to accommodate all our crinolines, but he drove us to the church. With relatively little additional fussing, we waited in the vestibule for things to begin. Today, the dressing of the bride has evolved into an ordeal. Since the bride is surrounded by an entourage of mothers, bridal consultants, coordinators, photographers, hairdressers, attendants, and the occasional well-wisher, any church being built today has to include a "bride's room" to accommodate this. The wedding industry that has blossomed in the past three decades has actually managed to influence church architecture!

EXPLAIN SOMETHING TO ME: The bride's *dress* is supposed to be a surprise for the groom, right? She comes mincing down the aisle all done up like a birthday present. The poor devil has to stand there checkin' her out. But what's the big deal? I'll betcha any money he's already seen what's inside!

I DON'T EVEN WANT TO look at my wedding pictures, because I hate my dress. I went dress shopping with my mom, my mother-in-law to be, and four aunts! That was just too many people and I was trying to please them all. They were totally into it. They coalesced into some weird collective—grown-up little girls all dressing me like they were playing dolls. Each of them forgot their individual taste and came up with this "greater mind." And I couldn't think for myself against that collection of possessed women. After trying on some seven dresses, I put one on and they all stood back and sighed: *That's* the one! So I took it. And I looked like Little Bo-Peep!

Groom's Attire

The bride wears a dress she may have dreamed of since childhood. She may have purchased it a year in advance. She wears it once and she may store it for years. The groom, on the other hand, may rent his clothes—tuxedo, slacks, shirt, tie, cummerbund, and shoes. The only things he wears to the wedding that are his own are his socks and underwear. He wears the rented outfit for a few hours and never thinks about it again. In comparison with the bride's attire, an imbalance quickly becomes apparent. What is this imbalance our culture fosters? The only thing the two have in common is that both the bride and groom spent a lot of money for the occasion. It is tempting to think that the wedding industry has been at work creating wants rather than satisfying needs.

A groom needs permission to reduce the escalating pressure that tells him what to wear. If a groom owns a suit, he could wear that. If he doesn't own one, it's time he did. Part of stepping over the threshold into marriage is also a stepping into the role of responsible adulthood. In our culture, a suit, even if it is not worn daily to work, is a symbol of adulthood and a commitment to taking that place in society. Most men could invest the money they would otherwise pay for a borrowed and uncomfortable tux into buying a suit that will have a more lasting value. It will give him a chance to express his taste and personality.

I WAS BEST MAN for my buddy's wedding. We went to a tux rental outfit downtown for fittings and suddenly had flashbacks of the last time we engaged in that racket. Senior prom, of course! We were just starting to tell each other our been-there-done-that story, when, sure enough, some kids arrived to pick out tuxes for a high school dance. Were we reenacting the same rite of passage? What's wrong with this picture? I'd say someone has us by the tail.

AT A PARISH RETREAT, the participants all had a chance to weave on a loom a collective effort. The fabric they wove would be fashioned into a stole for their presider and worn at the closing celebration. They brought fabric and cut thin strips of old dresses, shirts, tablecloths that had been used at significant times in their lives. They chatted away and remembered these various occasions or the people who had worn this cloth. There were bright scraps with many memories. There were bits of wedding dresses that showed up as well. One woman sat to the side in deep thought, looking at a handsome tie that she had spread out before her. Then she said that her husband had died only six weeks earlier. This was the tie he had worn when they married. "How fitting that this tie should now go to the altar again—as part of a stole—as part of the cloth that we all make together." Thoughtfully she began to cut the tie in narrow strips.

Wedding Attire for the Rest of the Party

Cause of romantic dreams—and even more consternation—is the dress of the attendants. What the attendants wear has no great symbolic value, although we have been programmed to believe that this fashion manifestation is vital—even central—to a wedding. A wedding is not a fashion show. The aisle is not a models' ramp.

Women don't come as matched sets. Nor should you choose your witnesses for their individual appearances or how they would look together. You choose them because they mean something

THE BRIDESMAIDS were all put into matching dresses, which, in turn, were a variation on the bride's. Very frilly and billowing with layers of netting. The dress worked for only one of the women, the bride's sister, and I'd be willing to wager she picked them out. One of the bridesmaids had a figure so much like my own—5'4" and, you know, kind of rotund—oh, Lordy. This was her shining moment, and, poor baby! I'm sorry, she looked like a gauze bowling ball.

FOR THE HONOR of being a bridesmaid several times over, I am now the proud owner of four god-awful dresses I wouldn't wear to a dogfight.

PEOPLE HAD TO BE EMBARRASSED when they saw the bridesmaids. What they wore would have looked more appropriate on a nightclub singer at a cheap bar: Slinky sheaths falling off the shoulder and slit up to here.

very special to you. Women have different figures and different tastes. Dresses chosen for them are often a serious strain to their budgets and hopelessly useless for later functions. Why not honor the individuality of your attendants and trust them. Consider asking your attendants to wear dresses of their choice, style, and design—with only, perhaps, a color preference or length suggested.

It is, of course, inappropriate to require mothers and grandmothers to enter into a prescribed color scheme.

You could also trust your male witnesses to dress appropriately, suggesting that they wear slacks and a blazer or a suit.

In a new era, concerned about the right value of things, we

can see that some of these practices that we are quick to call tradition or symbol may need our creative rethinking.

The Altar

When we speak of "going to the altar," we usually mean the act of getting married. If you marry in a church, you will very likely be married before an altar or a table. The altar has a many-layered meaning built up over the ages—from the rock of sacrifice, to the tomb built over the bones of ancestors, to the table of the Lord's own mysterious sacrificial meal, to the table around which we share our daily food. It is one of the focal points in the sanctuary and probably the oldest sacred symbol still part of our lives and worship.

In certain Christian religions, the altar is blessed, consecrated, and anointed with oil when the church is first dedicated. Not long ago, altars contained fragments of bone or relics from the "ancestors" deemed by the church to be saints. Surrounded by awe and mystery, for a long time only certain people could approach it. In Orthodox churches the altar and the action that takes place there are considered so sacred that they are hidden from public view behind a screen (called an *iconostasis*) painted with saints and angels.

Today the altar is still revered as something set apart from the ordinary tables of our daily use; people bow to it as they enter the church and the presider kisses it in greeting at the beginning of a service.

Some churches use a table and not an altar. They revere it as the table where the Lord's Supper is celebrated. The table underscores the holiness of our everyday experiences around the family table. Our daily meals are a kind of communion. Taking time around a table to share food, to talk, to negotiate, to be reconciled, to be nourished, makes every table something like an altar table in our homes, our consulting rooms, our conference rooms. The holiness of marriage becomes clear when you choose to "go to the altar."

The Cross

Long before the advent of Christianity, the cross was a symbol of life. Called the tree of life or the cosmic tree, its roots tapped into the depth of the earth and its branches rose to the heavens and spread out across the skies.

WHEN I WAS BAPTIZED, my godmother embroidered for me a fine white linen square with the date of my baptism. It was the cloth the priest used to dry my head. On the day I married, I used this baptismal cloth again on the altar. That symbolic cloth has been part of every major sacramental event in my life. When I die, I'd like that linen cloth to be the pall on my casket.

I HAD A RUSSIAN ORTHODOX WEDDING, complete with the bells ringing and a betrothal service at the rear of the church, marriage vows, crowns, shared wine, candles, and procession with hands tied together around the Gospels at the center of the church. We were presented with wedding icons. And then the blessing and the dismissal took place at the front of the church by the iconostasis. We gave each guest a card with an icon of Joachim and Anna and a prayer from the wedding blessing.

Christians revere the cross as a paradoxical symbol. As a symbol of life, it represents the fullness of life Christ promised to his followers. As a symbol of death, it reminds all who look upon it of the death Jesus suffered. The cross is a central symbol for Christianity, and you will find one in most churches.

On solemn occasions services often begin with a procession led by a crossbearer holding aloft a cross. It becomes the symbolic banner that leads everyone into the ceremony, sets its tone, and unites all disparate parts of the cosmos in healing and redemption. If you are celebrating your wedding in a vast outdoor place or a secular hall, consider borrowing a processional cross from a church. The cross will add a silent blessing to your gathering and give people a sense of the holiness of the occasion.

In many religious communities, worship services, including weddings, begin with the congregation making the "sign of the cross." Blessing themselves, from forehead to breast, from shoulder to shoulder, is a kind of centering gesture or a drawing together of the person in readiness for a sacred act.

The presider may also form a cross over both of you when the special nuptial blessing is given.

The Sacred Book and the Lectern

The Bible tells the sacred stories that are the basis of the Christian faith and of a Christian's identity. During worship services, as a sign of respect to the Word of God, it is venerated. Some churches proclaim the readings from a specially decorated or ornamental Bible, while others use a book of Scripture readings called the lectionary. Either way, it deserves special attention during the wedding. If you are using other books and readings from other sources, they will not be treated as sacred symbols as is the book of the Bible.

If you are having readings from Scripture, consider honoring the book (the Bible or the lectionary) in the entry procession. Together with the cross, presider, servers, and candles, the reader can enter with the rest, holding the book aloft for all to see. (For more on this, see the section on the entry procession.)

The Word is meant to be proclaimed, not just read aloud. It is read from a special location: the pulpit or the reader's stand. The reader's stand has a place of prominence in most churches equal to or exceeding the altar. It may be draped or otherwise honored to set it apart during a wedding ceremony.

If you marry in a setting other than a church, bring in a reader's stand—even a music stand will do—and set it in a special place, where the readers will proclaim the passages you have selected. Make it a special place, apart from the gathered community.

The Kiss

The kiss, within the context of a sacred ritual, is a universal sign of love, affection, peace, and greeting. In a wedding, the kiss that the bride and groom exchange is the kiss of peace. Traditionally—and the most meaningful manner in which this ritual is performed—the kiss passes from the presider to the bride and the groom. Then bride and groom embrace and kiss and pass the peace to their witnesses. Coming down from the altar, the bride and groom then pass the kiss of peace to their parents and families and, if they wish, up and down the aisle to their friends. Everyone in the assembly greets and passes the sign of peace

among themselves as well. Like a wildfire, the greeting and blessing of peace spreads around the assembly, as a handshake, an embrace, a kiss. This first kiss of the wife and husband is not meant
to be a public display of their sexual style. It belongs to all the
signs we spoke of earlier that denote harmony and unity for the
couple, for all the assembly and beyond all borders to the world.

Candles

A sacred action calls for candles. In this age of electricity we don't
need candles to light the way, but we cannot quite imagine a ceremony without that living flame. Candlelight flickers and moves
and casts a warm glow. It represents the energy and life of the
soul itself and of our shining, moving inner life. The flame leaps
up and bends to every breath of air. Especially for an evening or
night wedding, beyond the customary candles on the altar/table,
you may want to fill the place with candlelight.

The so-called unity candle is, however, a recent invention and
has quickly become the special province and promotion of the
florist who is glad to provide the accoutrements. Something of a
ritual has developed around the candles. The mothers of the
bride and groom or, sometimes, both their parents, light a candle before the ceremony begins. Then, after the couple has ex-
changed vows, the couple lights a single candle from the candles
their parents lit. It says—rather baldly—that the four parents
brought forth two lives and from those two lives a new one has
come into being.

This candle ritual simply restates what has already been richly
stated by other elements and actions of the ceremony. That statement was already acted out in the presentation of the couple by

---

I THINK THE BRIDE and groom got mixed up with their unity-candle thing! Each of their parents went up to the sanctuary and lit the two candles on either end of a five-branch candelabrum. Then the bride and groom got up with lots of precarious swishing of skirts, trains, and billowing veils. We had just gotten relaxed over the fact that she was safely gathered up and settled on her chair. They went up to the candelabrum, pulled up a burning candle each, used it to simultaneously light the middle candle, and then they blew out the four candles on either side! They just snuffed out their parents! I can't imagine that that was the idea of this thing—or—by gosh. *Was* it?

---

their parents. Through the exchange of the vows, a new creation has already been made. The unity candle and its ritual was probably invented to give the mothers something to do. It is right to honor and recognize them, but better by another means.

Only a lack of faith in the strength of what has already happened, loud and clear, produces a redundancy of this sort and spices it with a touch of sentimentality. The unity candle is simply that: redundant, a gilding of the lily, a symbolic Dagwood sandwich—symbols on top of symbols. Fill the place with candles if you wish, and allow them to flicker and burn without further comment.

Incense

Incense has always been a kind of "holy squandering." It serves no earthly purpose but represents only our willingness to "waste" what is precious to the glory of God. Made of precious resins

collected in the Middle East, its bright grains are laid on a glow-
ing coal, creating smoke that rises and curls and perfumes the air.
Sometimes incense is placed in a swinging censer to help send it
into the four corners or to swing it over what needs special blessing. You can also use a shallow bowl of smooth pebbles to set the
coal in. The bowl can then be carried in procession. Incense is a
symbol, too, of our prayers rising up—prayers that ask for nothing more than to be accepted as praise and thanksgiving.

In churches that use incense during their worship services, the
rites of incensing have a way of marking off a holy place and of
adding another blessing. You may want to incorporate incense
into your wedding by using it to lead in the procession, to bless
the altar, to bless the Bible or lectionary before the Gospel is read,
and to bless the rings. At an outdoor wedding, you can mark off
the place by blessing it with incense.

Water

Like the cross, water is a paradoxical symbol, signifying both life
and death. It can flood and drown living beings, and it can wash
what is dry and dusty. It can wreak havoc with flash floods and it
can bring life to an arid and thirsty land. It is the source and origin of all of life and continues to nurture us with thirst-quench-
ing, life-sustaining springs. The use of water during a worship
service recalls the life-giving waters of baptism. A water rite is
part of many sacramental celebrations. A sprinkling of holy water
over the people, the bride and groom, or, at the very least, over
the rings, is a way of blessing them.

MY WIFE'S FROM Minnesota and I'm your typical California surfer—but we always kidded each other about the "many waters we've been washed with." The Pacific Ocean and those Ten Thousand Lakes, just for starters. So we decided that the water that the rector blessed for our wedding should be a nice little mixture of Lake Minnetonka water and Pacific Ocean water. My mother-in-law brought us a jar of it when she came out for the wedding! It was this real subtle thing that meant something to us privately but got spread around publicly when the rector used it. She sprinkled and blessed our rings with it and then she sprinkled all the people with it too.

BECAUSE I'M AN AMATEUR wine maker, I asked our priest if we could use some of my best red wine for the Eucharist. He was very agreeable to the idea. My wife and her mother, then, offered to make a beautiful big round loaf of whole wheat bread. We each had our very favorite cousins bring our bread and wine forward as the gifts at the offertory. I tell you. Talk about symbols of transformation. That got to me! And I was thrilled to make that kind of contribution to the ceremony.

AN ACTION I found deeply moving was when the newly married couple served as Eucharistic ministers of communion, serving the community in a first act as husband and wife.

Food

In some churches (Roman Catholic, for example) weddings are often—though not always—celebrated in the context of the Eucharist. Celebrating the two events, marriage and the Eucharist, together is the Church's way of reminding the couple that their love for each draws its inspiration from the Lord's Supper. Just as bride and groom are the central symbol of marriage, so bread and wine are the main symbols of the Eucharist. This is my body, Jesus said. And in a marriage, you, too, give each other your bodies in sacred trust.

Flowers

It is the earth that gives us the flowers and plants that are so much a part of the wedding: the bouquet, a wreath, plants, trees, palms, or ferns that define the space. The addition of flower arrangements to a church should be simple and tasteful. Many parish churches have standards or principles for further decoration. Sometimes they allow only one central bouquet which they then ask be left for the week of services that take place in the church following the wedding. That means you will not be carrying that bouquet from the church to the reception.

The bride's bouquet is better when it doesn't distract from her own person, or become a major object for caretaking during the celebration. The bride might well want to tuck flowers that have personal meaning and symbolism for her into the bouquet. She may want to do the same with boutonnieres for the groom and groomsmen. But without further explanation, we can readily understand the flowers and leaves and fruits used throughout all aspects of the wedding celebration as gifts of nature and signs of fruitfulness and nature's beauty. At the end of the wedding, some brides pull up a blossom from their bouquet to give to each of the persons who have been especially significant to them—or just to family members.

When it comes to flowers, less is more. Instead of spending a fortune on them for your wedding, consider giving each other

---

FOR MY SISTER'S WEDDING, we cut branches of leaves from the local trees. You'd be surprised at how colorful foliage can be in mid-June! Burgundy, silver-gray, yellow, umpteen greens and variegated leaves, bright and dark. And we made arrangements that were stunning. Just leaves! In a certain few arrangements—those we made with mostly burgundy leaves from the decorative plum—we added pink and orange roses from our aunt's rose garden. We had more fun hunting up what was in season and what we could find in our several gardens just for the taking.

MY GRANDMA SAID that it was a tradition when she married—as it was for my great-grandmother—that the bride wear a wreath of myrtle. I looked it up and discovered that myrtle is "an emblem of love and sacred to Venus." I'm not sure she knew that. But I asked her to help my auntie make me a wreath with myrtle and lilies-of-the-valley. We wanted orange blossoms but we couldn't get any. Orange blossoms smell so good—and it's because they flower and fruit all at the same time that they are a fertility symbol. We used myrtle for the boutonnieres as well. Grandma really got into it. She was so happy to be part of things and to have had the idea.

flowers throughout your marriage. How much more enjoyable are those flowers spread out over the years—tokens of affection or reconciliation—than the flowers that overtaxed your budget and passed your notice in the blur of your wedding day.

———————

The sacred ceremony uses the basic elements of nature: earth, water, fire, and sustenance or nourishment. It is as though to say, all the works of the Lord, bless the Lord. Praise and exalt God forever and ever. Amen.

Music

Music is one of the languages of any good ritual. It speaks directly to the heart, bypassing our plodding reason. It allows us to feel and give voice to emotions so deep they elude articulation. In some ways music is like God: We can hear it but not grasp it, enjoy it but not contain it, experience it but not hold it still. It has the power to inspire, to stir the emotions, and to unite. A wedding would be incomplete without music.

Many churches have music directors who can provide valuable help in planning your ceremony. Music directors may also be the church's organist or chief soloist. They know the church's music policy. They know music and songs that are appropriate for a wedding, and ordinarily they coordinate and practice with guest instrumentalists or soloists, should you want to include these.

At a wedding, music serves three functions.

First, music gathers everyone present into a community and facilitates their participation in the ceremony. It quiets people, stirs them, or inspires them—not just individually but communally. One of the most effective ways of uniting disparate people and of involving them in a common action is to have them sing together. As they breathe in rhythm and sing together, they are united in spirit. (In many ancient languages the same word means both *breath* and *spirit*.)

Second, music adds solemnity and soul to a celebration. It sets the ritual's tone, the pacing, and the feel, lending it beauty and dignity. It tells people, not in a direct or didactic way, that a wedding ceremony is more than a celebration, it's worship.

Finally, music serves the ceremony itself. It is integral to the ritual, as essential to its functioning as words, gestures, and symbols. Within more formal church weddings, certain rites are meant to be sung.

Consider asking the assembled people to sing. Songs and hymns do their own work at a wedding; they unite the people in a common action and engage them emotionally and spiritually. To encourage people to sing, choose songs that are familiar and uncomplicated. The hymnal used by your church is a good place to begin. It is appropriate to sing songs of praise for the love God bestows—while love songs, show tunes, and popular music are more suitable to the reception.

It is more important to have an experienced song leader than an accomplished soloist at your wedding. Song leaders do what their name suggests, they lead others—your guests—in singing. While they often are accomplished singers themselves, they are more committed to drawing others into participation than to drawing attention to themselves by performing. Soloists or solo performances, unfortunately, contribute to keeping a congregation passive and waiting to be entertained. You want music and musicians to involve people so deeply in what is happening that they don't even have the chance to express admiration for a performance.

The organ is the preeminent instrument at most church weddings since it is capable of producing the rich power and volume necessary to fill a church and to give the people the courage to sing out. For more informal ceremonies, however, you may want to draw from any number of different combinations: piano and organ, flute and oboe, violin and flute, piano and harp, piano and violin, or violin and cello. A guitar and bass, a single trumpet, a brass quartet, or a woodwind ensemble are also possible. If you are planning a very formal wedding, you might consider engaging a choir or small group of singers. Keep in mind, however, that the music—in addition to being beautiful—must serve both the congregation and the service.

Many churches have an arrangement with their organist, stating that he or she is to be used at all weddings performed in that particular church. If you want to bring in your own musicians, you may be asked to pay the organist a "bench fee" (a sum of money for *not* playing).

Outdoor weddings, because of the lack of acoustics, pose a

special challenge for musicians. The open air swallows sound, and all but the loudest music has little chance of being heard by everyone present. An electric keyboard is one possibility. Better ones, which can be rented for the occasion, produce a remarkably high quality sound and sufficient volume for most open air settings. If you have arranged for vocalists to sing, do them, your guests, and yourselves a favor: Rent a sound system with microphones, an amplifier, and speakers.

Recorded music is the least satisfying solution. Too frequently the sound reproduction and the volume are second-rate—especially if you rely on portable players. Recorded music also encourages passivity and discourages participation. In a church setting it would be better to do without music altogether than to play music over the sound system. (Many denominations explicitly prohibit the use of prerecorded music for worship.) A single guitar and vocalist, with amplification, can provide music that serves the celebration better.

––––––

At most weddings music is used in the background for guests to listen to while waiting for the ceremony to begin or as an accompaniment for some action, like the seating of important guests. It is also used as a fanfare to mark the entrance procession and the recessional. But music has other functions in a wedding that shouldn't be overlooked.

Music can be used for the different parts of the ceremony:

- *Organ preludes—literally, music "played before"—can provide a sense of peace while your guests arrive and are seated.*

- *An ensemble can play softly before the wedding begins, tapering off just as the last guests are seated.*
- *A solo before the processional can quiet your guests and mentally prepare them for what is about to happen.*
- *The processional greets the wedding party. It can be an instrumental selection or a joyful hymn sung by everyone present. Since most people seem intent on watching the procession, it may be futile to ask them to sing at that time. You might want to process in to instrumental music and then, once you are standing before everyone, have people sing a hymn of praise together.*
- *A psalm can be sung following the first reading. There are many musical settings for the psalms, which from their conception were always sung.*
- *An alleluia can be sung before the reading of the gospel.*
- *If you do choose to light a "unity candle," instrumental music works best.*
- *A solo or, better yet, a hymn of praise can be sung after the speaking of vows and exchange of rings.*
- *The Lord's Prayer should never be sung by a soloist. For centuries this has been the preeminent prayer that brings people together. On a practical level, it is one of the few prayers that just about everyone knows. If everyone present knows a musical setting to the Lord's Prayer, you might want to have them sing it. Otherwise, it is best simply to have people speak it.*
- *The recessional—again, an instrumental or a congregational hymn—sends you and the whole wedding party out of the church on a happy, lively note.*
- *Spirited music can be played as a postlude as your guests leave.*

College and university libraries and most large city libraries maintain music departments with recordings you can either check out or listen to in special booths.

Musical Suggestions

PRELUDES:

BACH, JOHANN SEBASTIAN
Abide with Us, Lord Jesus Christ
Adagio
Jesu, Joy of Man's Desiring
Sheep May Safely Graze
Sleepers Awake

BOËLLMANN, LÉON
Suite Gothique

BRAHMS, JOHANNES
Behold, a Rose Is Blooming
My Jesus Calls to Me

BUXTEHUDE, DIETRICH
Organ Works

ELMORE, ROBERT
Three Meditative Moments Based on Moravian Hymns

HANDEL, GEORGE FRIDERIC
Adagio in E from Violin Sonata
Air from Water Music Suite
Aria in F major

HAYDN, FRANZ JOSEPH
The Musical Clocks

MENDELSSOHN, FELIX
  Consolation
  On Wings of Song
PACHELBEL, JOHANN
  Canon
PEETERS, FLOR
  Now Thank We All Our God
  Wedding Song
PURCELL, HENRY
  Bell Symphony
  Voluntary in C major
VIVALDI, ANTONIO
  Spring from The Four Seasons
WIDOR, CHARLES-MARIE
  Symphony No. 5—Part IV

VOCAL WORKS
  BACH, JOHANN SEBASTIAN
    Be Thou But Near
    Jesu, Joy of Man's Desiring
  BEETHOVEN, LUDWIG VAN
    Joyful, Joyful We Adore Thee
    When Thou Art Near
  DUNGAN, OLIVE
    Eternal Life (Prayer of St. Francis of Assisi)
  DVOŘÁK, ANTONIN
    Biblical Songs, Book I
    God Is My Shepherd
    I Will Sing New Songs of Gladness

FRANCK, CÉSAR AUGUSTE

Panis Angelicus (O Lord Most Holy)

GRIEG, EDVARD

Ich Liebe Dich (So Love I Thee)

MENDELSSOHN, FELIX

A Wedding Prayer

Consolation

If with All Your Hearts

MOZART, WOLFGANG AMADEUS

Alleluia

PAGE, S. E.

The Love of God Flows Deep and Strong

SCHUBERT, FRANZ

Ave Maria

SCHÜTZ, HEINRICH

Wedding Prayer

Wedding Song

VAUGHAN WILLIAMS, RALPH

A Wedding Prayer

PROCESSIONALS:

BACH, JOHANN SEBASTIAN

Adagio from Toccata in C major

Fantasy in G major (middle section)

Jesu, Joy of Man's Desiring

Sinfonia from Wedding Cantata

BEETHOVEN, LUDWIG VAN

Ode to Joy

BLOCH, ERNEST

Four Wedding Marches

BRAHMS, JOHANNES
St. Anthony's Chorale
Variations on a Theme by Haydn

CLARK, JEREMIAH
Trumpet Voluntary

HANDEL, GEORGE FRIDERIC
Air from Water Music Suite
Aria in F major
Solemn Processional from Water Music Suite
Thanks Be to Thee

PURCELL, HENRY
Trumpet Tune in D major
Trumpet Voluntaire
Praise, My Soul, the King of Heaven

TELEMANN, GEORG PHILIPP
Concerto in A minor

HYMNS SUCH AS:
Praise to the Lord, the Almighty

PSALMS AND ALLELUIAS

The psalms most appropriate for a wedding are 33, 34, 103, 112, 121, 128, and 145. Unlike the other titles listed here, musical settings for psalms and alleluias are not published separately. The best place to find them is in the church's hymnal, although you can find or purchase any of these fine collections of psalms:

The Psalter, *John Knox Press, Louisville, Ky.*
Psalms for Feasts and Seasons, *Christopher Wilcock, The Liturgical Press, Collegeville, Minn.*

Psalms for the Cantor, *Volumes I-VI, World Library
Publications, Inc., Schiller Park, Ill.*
Psalms and Selected Canticles, *Robert E. Kreutz,
OCP Publications, Portland, Oreg.*

Alleluias are not published in collections in the way psalms are.
They are found mainly in hymnals or otherwise as part of entire
Mass settings.

RECESSIONALS AND POSTLUDES:
  BEETHOVEN, LUDWIG VAN
    Ode to Joy
  HANDEL, GEORGE FRIDERIC
    Allegro Maestoso from Water Music Suite
    Hornpipe from Water Music Suite
    Postlude in G major
    Processional in G major
    The Rejoicing from Peace Music
  MENDELSSOHN, FELIX
    Wedding March from Midsummer Night's Dream
  PURCELL, HENRY
    Bell Symphony
    Trumpet Voluntary in D major
    Trumpet Tune in D major
  SOLER, ANTONIO
    The Emperor's Fanfare
  WILLAN, JAMES H.
    Finale Jubilante

HYMNS SUCH AS:

Joyful, Joyful We Adore Thee
Love Divine, All Loves Excelling
Now Thank We All Our God
Praise to the Lord the Almighty

2

The Ceremony and Reception

The Rites of Gathering

At your invitation, people come from the many places and periods in your lives. Old family friends and relatives you haven't seen for years arrive, perhaps from far away. Friends and coworkers who have never met one another come too. They arrive in one place, and it is the function of a good ritual to unite them, if only temporarily, in spirit and intention.

The rite of gathering is the name given to the first part of the wedding ceremony. It includes everything that assembles the guests and begins the service: actions, words, gestures, music, and decorations. It gathers the people, forms them into a community, and prepares them for what is about to happen. Practically, this includes three movements: the process of assembling people, the entry procession, and the presider's opening greeting, remarks, and prayer.

Assembling Your Guests

The first and most basic step in the gathering rite is to assemble everyone in the same place—to get them to the church, the home, the hotel, the park, or that place in nature where the ceremony will take place—and then to seat or arrange them as you wish. It is, in essence, a ritual of *welcoming*.

Welcoming begins long before the day of the wedding, since you actually gathered people to your side from the moment you first announced your engagement. Then you compile a guest list, and you design and mail out invitations. There are any number of social functions to attend or host: the introductory meeting of your two families, showers, and most important the rehearsal dinner. At every step, more and more people invest themselves emotionally, physically, and financially in your wedding. Getting your friends and family fully involved begins the process of welcoming.

Finding the Way

On the day of the wedding, you continue the process of welcoming your guests by making it as easy as possible for them to find their way to the right place. For this, you include directions or maps with the invitations. You could further mark the place, especially if it is difficult to find, with bright banners or wind socks. For an evening wedding you could illuminate the place with garden torches or line the walkways with luminarias—candles in an open, sand-filled paper bag.

You Are the Hosts

Greeting people as they arrive, the most fundamental step in welcoming your guests, sets the tone for much of what is to follow. In spite of what most wedding etiquette books imply, there is no single, obligatory way to greet your guests. You can create your own manner of welcoming them, according to your personalities and style. The important thing is: *What* you do is less important than *how* you do it.

As the bride and groom, you are the hosts of this celebration. Consider greeting the people yourselves as they enter, introducing them to each other, or passing them along to others who will seat them. Keeping the bride hidden from the groom and the guests until the very last moment interferes with this gesture of welcome and hospitality. There is little reason to keep the bride's attire a secret. Involve your attendants and witnesses in the wedding party—women and men—in greeting the guests and seating them. Or ask certain friends and family members who have no other part in the ceremony to perform this function, asking them to make a special effort to be warmly welcoming and hospitable. If you greet people yourselves, you may want to take a moment right before the ceremony begins to collect your thoughts and to prepare yourselves inwardly for what you are about to do.

Rarely do couples continue the custom of separating guests along "party affiliation"—bride's or groom's—seating them on different sides of the aisle. Whatever its historical origin, the custom runs counter to what you want to accomplish: bringing your guests together.

Although you reserve the front row or two for immediate family members, it makes good sense to usher everyone else as close to the front as possible. Seating people in a close group increases both their sense of belonging to a community and their likelihood of participating. If people are physically scattered, a few people in each row, they will also feel emotionally disconnected.

Most probably your guests will be unfamiliar with the church or physical setting and will want to look around and get situated. People should feel free to speak to the others around them and get acquainted. Appropriate music in the background sets the tone and invites people to make their transitions and "arrive" on every level. They settle in, feel oriented and connected, and look forward to the wedding.

The Procession

The second movement of the gathering rite is the procession.

For all its formality and fanfare, the procession simply moves you from one place to another, from the entrance of the church to the altar.

Of course, it also operates on a much deeper, more symbolic level. It signifies your journey as a couple. Outwardly you walk down the aisle with family and friends looking on, a passage of only a few minutes. But inwardly you are undertaking a much longer journey, enacting a transition from one way of life to another. As the procession moves you from the church's entrance to its altar or the center of the ceremonies, it is your love that

STANDING JUST BEFORE the wedding ceremony begins, at the sacred thresh-old itself, take time, each of you, to examine the tension you are feeling. Given the gravity of the moment, some of this tension is entirely appropriate! But you also want to be fully present for your own wedding and not so wrapped in a fog of anxiety that you can barely attend to the moment. Gather yourselves together. Fold your hands. Close your eyes. Breathe deeply. With every breath you take in, feel the fresh, clean air fill your whole being. Exhale deeply. While you exhale, drop your shoulders from up there around your ears, where you are probably holding them. Every time you exhale, drop them lower still. Relax your tongue and jaw. Allow all your joints to "unhinge" their tensions. Breathe in and out. Let go. Offer yourselves to a loving and gracious God who has brought you to this day and to this holy moment.

moves you from love's entrance to its most sacred core. By the time you take your place, you will feel as if you have taken a very long journey. And you have. You have walked through the entire length of your relationship, realizing and reliving, in a very short time, everything, from courtship to the commitment that has brought you to this moment.

As a sign of love's journey, the procession draws other people into its path. Families and friends stand, as if in silent homage to the love they are witnessing, and they turn to face you with expectation and feeling. They fix their eyes on you. As you walk by, they change their positions to keep you in sight, just as they will now all have to change the way they relate to you. During the brief moments of the procession, you carry their hopes and good wishes and everyone is moved with feeling. That first chord of processional music often brings the first tears that weddings inevitably elicit. Your transition marks and effects a change in them. Before this entrance they were little more than a group of diverse people gathered in a single place. By the completion of the procession they become a community united in focus and intention. The custom of the bride processing down the aisle preceded by various children and her attendants and escorted by her father does questionable justice to the full meaning and purpose of this profound moment. While children deserve to be present and a part of the ceremony, they aren't honored by being put on display and trained to perform. With women attendants nervously taking short steps and feigning bright smiles in their fear, it often resembles more a fashion runway than a procession. Arriving on the arm of her father, the bride reenacts an outdated, even paternalistic view of women as extensions, if not possessions, of men. Thought incapable of standing on her own, a woman in other civilizations and in times past remained under the protection and rule of a man, first of her father, and then of her husband. That older form of bridal procession enacted this "transfer of goods" as the bride's father handed her over to the new man in her life, the man who would next exercise authority over her. That the woman is being handed over from one man to another is made explicit in the question that often marked the culmination of the procession: "Who gives this woman in marriage?"

The noted psychiatrist Carl Jung suggested, however, that the custom of the father "giving away" the bride served a symbolic function: It said that the woman had to relinquish her "parental images" in order to enter an adult relationship to her husband in marriage.

WHEN I TALK TO THE BRIDE and groom about the procession, they often seem surprised that they don't have to do it "the traditional way." They thought that the church required them to do it that way.

NO WAY. I just tell the kids, no "giving away." That's not the way we do it in the church. Period.

I FIND A GOOD FIFTY PERCENT of the young people who come to the church to be married are very agreeable—even enthusiastic—about making some adjustments in their initial expectations if I just take the time to help them think it through. When I don't have the time to lead them through it, that's when they resist.

MY WIFE SAID, "Don't ask me to come down the aisle with you to give our daughter away! You're her dad and you have to give her away. Your relationship with her is the one that's going to change. Not mine. I'll never have to give her away because our relationship is not going to change. We'll always be close." You know, my wife may be surprised by how much the mother-daughter relationship will need to change after the marriage.

The bride's mother, so important in her daughter's life, seems to have little or nothing to say in the matter.

The bridal procession not only undervalues the bride's dignity and ignores her mother's role, it also shortchanges the groom's role. While everyone turns to face the bride, the groom quietly waits in the wings with his attendants, as if not wanting to draw attention to himself. It says that his route to this important moment is less important and transforming than hers. It says that his family has no part in the matter. And, if Jung is right about the bride needing to let go of her parental images, what of the groom and his need?

Miss Manners asks why the bride needs to be given away while the groom just donates himself.

———

Couples dissatisfied with the symbolism of the above bridal procession have reframed this manner of entry or discarded it entirely. Some have retrieved a more ancient custom—a variation still practiced in Jewish weddings. Here, both bride and groom are escorted down the aisle between their fathers and mothers and surrounded by their witnesses. Such a procession honors all the parents and recognizes the bride and groom as equal partners.

You have arrived at this moment—both of you—not on your own as fully formed from the hand of God, but guided and supported most especially by those who gave you birth: Your mother and your father. Since they never really owned you, they

NO MATTER what you call it, that trip down the aisle is a giving-away. It was a chance for us to think about the end of our relationship with our daughter and the beginning of a new relationship with a son-in-law. He was given away, too, by his mother and father. We were all moved by that.

do not give you away. Rather, they give you one more demonstration of love, the gift of letting you go—handing you on—so that you may love and be loved by another.

Given the nature of families and the fact of divorce and stepparents, you may have to consider carefully before deciding who will accompany you down the aisle. Ask, "Who is important and took part in bringing me to this moment?" For many it will be their father and mother. For some it will be one parent and a stepparent or two parents and their spouses. For others it will be a much larger family, including perhaps brothers and sisters, grandparents, aunts, and uncles. For still others it will be children from a previous marriage. Whoever they are, the way you know them is by their history of loving you.

Many women, independent in every other way, have always imagined being escorted down the aisle by their fathers and can imagine no other way of doing it. And some fathers have always seen this moment as their privilege and duty; they would be bewildered or feel left out if their role were altered. If this is the case for you, relax. Enjoy the moment. You can reframe your

---

MY MOTHER'S GOING BALLISTIC because my dad, from whom she's been divorced since I was seven, is going to walk me down the aisle. She figures she and my stepdad raised me and either one of them should walk me down the aisle. I can see her point, but my dad has taken it so for granted that this was his role, and he was so looking forward to this moment, that I'm actually using "tradition" as an excuse to make up our minds for us. I can't imagine what I'd unleash if I changed things around now. Bad enough having my mom mad at me, but I think hurting my dad, at this point, would be even harder to deal with.

understanding of the procession so that you are presented to the groom, not given away.

There is no reason you cannot be escorted by someone other than your father. If he is no longer living or has removed himself from your life, you are free to ask any other person to be your escort: your mother, a brother, a sister, an uncle, your stepfather, your godmother.

I HAD MY BROTHER give me away, but I look at this differently, maybe because I never really had a father. I see marriage as joining the individuals but also their families. So I wanted a representative from my family involved. Since I couldn't possibly choose among my five sisters, I asked my only brother. It was really great walking hand in hand with him—recognizing that I wouldn't be where I am today without my family. Each kid in my family chose to do this differently. One of my sisters wanted Mom to escort her down the aisle, but she refused, so my sister went down alone.

Varieties of Wedding Procession

There are many ways to arrange a more inclusive procession. But first, begin by calling it a *wedding* procession and not a *bridal* procession.

- *The presider stands before the altar. The attendants, male and female, walk in, two by two. The groom enters, escorted by his parents and/or family. Finally, the bride processes in, similarly escorted.*
- *The presider leads the procession preceded by a crossbearer, al-*

tar servers (carrying candles), and/or reader (carrying the book). They are followed by the groomsmen and bridesmaids, the groom with his family, and the bride with hers.

- *The procession begins with a person holding an incensor (a flat bowl with incense grains burning on top of lit charcoal) or a church's swinging censer and another person carrying a processional cross. A reader holding aloft the book of readings precedes the presider. The attendants follow (preferably clustered), then the groom with his family and the bride with hers.*

- *The two of you could walk in together at the end of the procession, with your parents or families in front of you.*

- *In places without—or arranged without—a central aisle, the groom and his family process in from one side while the bride and her family process in from the other. They meet in the middle before the presider.*

- *In outdoor settings a "meeting of clans" may be more appropriate. The groom walks with his family and friends as the bride walks with her family and friends, from opposite places to the central gathering place. The presider welcomes them in the middle. Everyone else takes her and his seat.*

LISTEN, some of those old rules of etiquette have had their day. Things have changed too much between the sexes. Our wedding was in a friend's garden. We had a no-aisle wedding. I didn't want to be "given away" by my father, and we didn't want the asymmetry of a center aisle for the bride and the wings for the groom. My father, however, not having had a role in walking me in, really felt he should give a speech. So he did. He wrote out this little sermon on marriage and he gave it during the ceremony. It was really rather sweet.

The Greeting

Now the two of you stand before the presider. When the processional music ends, after a brief pause the presider addresses you and the assembled guests. His or her intention is to set the tone for the ceremony, to explain its intent, and to prepare everyone present for what is about to happen.

In more formal liturgical ceremonies the presider may welcome everyone with a standard greeting such as "The Lord be with you" or "The grace and peace of our Lord Jesus Christ be with you" or simply "Peace be with you." In such a case, the response is "And also with you."

The presider may speak more informally, with words of his or her own choosing, welcoming you all and stating the reason for the occasion. "Informal" does not mean casual, breezy, or unplanned. Here are several examples:

- *We have gathered here today to witness the marriage vows of _____ and _____. We, their family and friends, form a community of love that together we may support them with our prayers and blessings.*
- *Dearly beloved, we are assembled here in the presence of God, to join this man and this woman in holy marriage. Let us, therefore, pray for their well-being and happiness.*
- *Beloved, let us love one another, for love is of God, and those who love are born of God and know God. Let us join together in love to witness the marriage vows of _____ and _____.*

Depending on your comfort and ease before people, you might want to add your own greeting to the presider's. You could thank everyone for coming, introduce members of your family, and, possibly, ask everyone to take a moment to introduce themselves to the people around them. (If you are going to do this, be sure to speak loudly enough for everyone to hear. You should consider using a microphone, depending on the size of the gathering space.)

The Charge

Following the greeting, the presider may make a statement, called a charge, about the nature and responsibilities of marriage.

The charge, common to many Protestant ceremonies (and to the old Roman Catholic ceremony), is an instruction and admonition. Addressed either to everyone assembled or more directly to the two of you, it reflects on the nature, purpose, and demands of marriage and either directly or indirectly challenges you to live up to the commitment you are undertaking. It says, in effect, this is what marriage is; are you sure you want to undertake it? Here are some examples:

- *I require and charge you both, as you stand in the presence of God, before whom the secrets of all hearts are disclosed, that, having duly considered the holy covenant you are about to make, you do now declare before this company your pledge of faith, each to the other. Be well assured that if these solemn vows are kept inviolate, as God's worth demands, and if steadfastly you endeavor to do the will of your heavenly Father, God will bless your marriage, will grant you fulfillment in it, and will establish your home in peace. (Methodist)*
- *Dearly beloved: We have come together in the presence of God*

to witness and bless the joining together of this man and this woman in holy matrimony. The bond and covenant of marriage was established by God in creation, and our Lord Jesus Christ adorned this manner of life by His presence and first miracle at a wedding in Cana of Galilee. It signifies to us the mystery of the union between Christ and His Church, and holy Scripture commends it to be honored among all people. The union of husband and wife in heart, body, and mind is intended by God for their mutual joy; for the help and comfort given one another in prosperity and adversity; and, when it is God's will, for the procreation of children, and their nurture in the knowledge and love of the Lord. Therefore marriage is not to be entered into unadvisedly or lightly, but reverently, deliberately, and in accordance with the purposes for which it was instituted by God. (Episcopal)

- *We are gathered here in the sight of God and of God's Church that this man and this woman may be joined together in holy matrimony, which is an honorable estate, which God has instituted and blessed, and by which God gives us a picture of the very communion of Christ and His Bride, the Church. God has both established and sanctified this estate and has promised to bless therein all who love and trust in God and who seek to give God their faithful worship and service, for the sake of our Lord Jesus Christ. God has ordained marriage for the good of man and woman in lifelong companionship according to God's good pleasure and that children may be nurtured to the praise of God's holy name. God has further ordained marriage so that the love you have for each other may be hallowed and fulfilled according to God's bountiful purposes, both in prosperity and adversity all your days. (Lutheran)*

- *The Bible teaches that marriage is to be a permanent relationship of one man and one woman freely and totally committed to each other as companions for life. Our Lord declared that man shall leave his father and mother and unite with his wife in the building of a home, and the two shall become one flesh. (Baptist)*
- *This union, then, is most serious, because it will bind you together for life in a relationship so close and so intimate that it will profoundly influence your whole future. That future, with its hopes and disappointments, its successes and its failures, its pleasures and its pains, its joy and its sorrows, is hidden from your eyes. You know that these elements are mingled in every life and are to be expected in your own. And so, not knowing what is before you, you take each other for better or for worse, for richer or for poorer, in sickness and in health, until death. (Roman Catholic)*

The Prayer

An opening prayer usually concludes the gathering rite.

The call to prayer could be the simple ritual invitation many churches use: "Let us pray." Or it could be less formal: "As we join in asking God's blessing on _____ and _____, let us bow our heads in prayer" or "As _____ and _____ begin a new step in their lives together, we pause in silence to pray."

Let silence follow the invitation so that people have time enough to pull together their own thoughts and to form their own prayers. At first they might shift about and make restless noises, but soon enough they will settle into the silence and be quiet together. The silence of prayer, almost palpable, will deepen the unity of everyone involved.

If you are being married in a church that uses its own prayer book, discuss the various prayers with your presider. Often the book suggests several different prayers. Ask your presider to read them aloud to you so that the three of you can decide together which prayer best articulates what you would like said at your wedding.

If your presider is open to the possibility, you might want to compose your own prayer which he or she would pray at the right moment.

Here are a variety of prayers from different traditions that might serve as models for your own prayer.

- *O Lord of life and love,*
  bestow your grace upon this marriage,
  and seal this commitment of your children with your love.
  As you have brought them together by your divine providence,
  sanctify them by your spirit,
  that they may give themselves fully one to the other and to
      you.
  Give them strength and patience to live their lives
  in a manner that will mutually bless themselves
  and honor your holy name;
  through Jesus Christ our Lord. Amen. (Baptist)
- *O gracious and everliving God,*
  you have created us male and female in your image.
  Look mercifully upon this man and this woman
  who come to you seeking your blessing,
  and assist them with your grace,
  that with true fidelity and steadfast love
  they may honor and keep the promises and vows they make;

through Jesus Christ our savior,
who lives and reigns with you in the unity of the Holy Spirit,
one God, for ever and ever. Amen. *(Episcopal)*

• *Almighty God,*
hear our prayers for _____ *and* _____,
who have come here today
to be united in the sacrament of marriage.
Increase their faith in you and in each other,
and through them bless your church.
We ask you this
through our Lord Jesus Christ, your son,
who lives and reigns with you and the Holy Spirit,
one God, for ever and ever. (Roman Catholic)

• *Eternal God, our creator and redeemer,*
as you gladdened the wedding at Cana in Galilee
by the presence of your son,
so by his presence now bring your joy to this wedding.
Look in favor upon _____ *and* _____
and grant that they, rejoicing in all your gifts,
may at length celebrate with Christ the marriage feast
which has no end. (Lutheran)

From the moment the procession begins through the prayer, everyone remains standing. Their attention has shifted as their eyes followed you to the front of the gathering space, and they have gradually been formed into a community, united in thought and prayer. Following the "amen," everyone sits, ready for what follows.

The Readings—an Overview

In most church wedding ceremonies the gathering rite is followed by Scripture readings and the minister's reflection (the sermon or homily). This part of the service is called by various names—the Liturgy of the Word, the Ministry of the Word, or simply the Word—but, whatever its name, it has one purpose. It provides the spiritual context for what you are about to do. It reminds you and the assembled people that your love and marriage is rooted in the mystery of God's own love.

In a simple ceremony this section may be little more than the minister reading a sentence or two from Scripture and then commenting on it. In other ceremonies there may be as many as three Scripture readings: one from the Old Testament or Hebrew Scripture, one from the Epistles, and one from the Gospels (in that order). More typically there are two readings: one from either the Old Testament or the Epistles and one from the Gospels.

Since the readings you select for the ceremony set the tone and lay out a spiritual conception of marriage as you want to frame it, you will want to choose them with care.

I REALLY BALK at young people wanting nonscripture readings at their weddings and I rarely allow it. But the best nonbiblical reading experience I had was when I was chaplain at SW. An elderly grandma, a doppelgänger of actress Ruth Gordon, wearing a cape (violet, I think) and a hat to match, did a reading of the "Intellectual Lover" about two old coots meeting in a bar and one telling the story of all his conquests—at twenty-one, at thirty, at forty, etc. The punch line was they were all the same woman, his wife!! Better yet, the story was written by the groom's grandfather and the woman who read it with much brio (and at age seventy-five still taught in the drama school) was the woman. My point is that a nonscriptural piece should be embedded in the family experience, not something dumped artily or otherwise by a clergyperson or a couple on the guests.

In the past, the readings at wedding ceremonies were invariably drawn from the Bible. Today, as couples take a more active role in planning their ceremonies, you can never be quite sure what you are going to hear. A poem, perhaps. Or a contemporary author's reflection on love and marriage. Or a passage from the Scriptures of another spiritual tradition.

Consult with the person performing your wedding. Many, if

GIVEN WHO I AM, I think weddings that try to be cute or "eclectic" are usually a bore and generally reflect too privatized a notion of marriage. How dare anyone think they have discovered marriage, or love or commitment. As we both know it is tradition (and Scripture readings) that helps us to see and understand and celebrate such awesome transitional moments . . . not just the bride and groom's transition either.

not most, ministers and churches will require you to select your readings solely from the Bible. They consider Scripture readings to be a fundamental element of any religious ceremony, as essential to a wedding's integrity as the prayers, vows, and blessing.

Your minister will probably give you a list of readings from the Bible that are appropriate for a wedding and encourage you to choose one or more of them for your wedding. (We include a selection of readings below.) Take your time while making your choice. You will want to choose words that describe what is best about your love and that challenge you to grow even stronger in your commitment and sharing.

Read the passages out loud to each other and reflect on them together, prayerfully. Use the readings as a way of meditating on your lives, on your love. What does each reading say about love? About the sacrifices demanded by love and the rewards offered by it? About the role played by faithfulness and forgiveness in love? And about the next step the two of you are taking together?

If you marry in a nonchurch setting, and depending on the person performing your service, you may have more freedom in selecting your readings. A love poem that is out of place in a church may sound just the right note at a small gathering in the

COMPARE VARIOUS translations of the Bible. Most versions are similar (especially contemporary ones), but each has its distinct style. You may find one more moving than the others, more beautiful, more powerful or poetic. As a means of comparison, consider these translations of Paul's meditation on love in First Corinthians, Chapter Thirteen:

King James Version:
Charity suffereth long, and is kind; charity envieth not; charity vaunteth not itself, is not puffed up. Doth not behave itself unseemly, seeketh not her own, is not easily provoked, thinketh no evil; Rejoiceth not in iniquity, but rejoiceth in the truth.

The New Jerusalem Bible:
Love is always patient and kind; love is never jealous; love is not boastful or conceited, it is never rude and never seeks its own advantage, it does not take offense or store up grievances. Love does not rejoice at wrongdoing, but finds its joy in the truth.

The New American Bible:
Love is patient, love is kind. It is not jealous, [love] is not pompous; it is not inflated; it is not rude, it does not seek its own interests, it is not quick-tempered, it does not brood over injury, it does not rejoice over wrongdoing but rejoices with the truth.

The Revised English Bible:
Love is patient and kind. Love envies no one, is never boastful, never conceited, never rude; love is never selfish, never quick to take offense. Love keeps no score of wrongs, takes no pleasure in the sins of others, but delights in the truth.

woods. Nonetheless, take care making your selection. The words spoken at your wedding must be as powerful and profound as the other elements of your wedding.

As you make your selections consider the following:

PUBLIC — How will this passage sound when it is proclaimed to the number of people you expect at your wedding? Will all the people you have invited be able to understand it on the first hearing?

A reading at a wedding ceremony is public in two ways:

It is public in that it is proclaimed to a number of different people at the same time.

We are not accustomed to being read to and listening. Many of us find it hard to understand new material when it is read to us, especially if it is complicated in any way. If we are read to for much longer than a minute or two, many tend to lose interest or stop listening. Be sure, then, to choose something that all the many different people you have gathered at your wedding are capable of understanding on first hearing.

The reading is also public as in "not private." Words that the

---

WE MET OVER POETRY in a lit class, and as we became romantically involved, we started reading our favorite poets or plays to each other. When we got engaged, we knew we wanted our favorite poetry to be part of our wedding. We chose a piece we felt everyone would agree was perfect for the occasion. We were excited about the idea, but frankly, it didn't work. A lot of people simply didn't understand it. They asked me later to explain the reading. And it did feel strange hearing it read to a church full of people, many of whom either she or I didn't know. It felt awkward. It didn't fly.

---

two of you share in your intimate moments—true and powerful as they may be—usually do not translate well into public celebrations.

COMMUNAL—Does this reading draw from the shared heritage of the community you have gathered to witness your wedding? Is it familiar (meaning "of the family") to your guests in meaning or tone or wording? Does it establish a common ground among your guests?

If your guests hear a reading at your wedding that they have heard at other weddings—maybe even at their own—they will feel more connected to you and to each other.

PROFOUND—Is the reading significant and substantive, solid enough for people to mull over and reflect on?

Even if you are planning a casual ceremony—or maybe *especially* if you are—the reading should be significant. Give your guests something to think about, something that ushers them into reflection. Since the readings are a commentary of sorts on your love for each other, avoid anything that is lightweight, frivolous, or trivial.

TRANSCENDENT—Is the reading capable of leading you beyond your current understanding of life and love and the demands your commitment will make on you? Does it open you to the possibility of learning more about love than you know now?

In the end, love remains a mystery, richer and deeper, fuller and more demanding than can easily be comprehended. That's why the reading you choose has to be big enough and wide enough and deep enough to hold something of that mystery. In a few years, when your love has been polished with use and time, will that reading sound old or tinny or inadequate to your acquired experience?

WE'VE BEEN MARRIED seventeen years, and I'm still moved by one of the readings from our wedding. It's the one where St. Paul says to put on heartfelt compassion, to bear with one another, and to forgive each other's faults. We both liked the reading then, but I never imagined how much it would mean to us now. Whenever we go through a rough time, between ourselves or with one of our kids, I go back to that reading. Each time I find more and more wisdom in it, and derive more courage. It's a keeper!

TIMELESS—Does the reading express a timeless truth? Does it continue to seem fresh and wise over the ages?

In literature a *classic* is a text that expresses something fundamental, something profoundly true about the human condition in words that come alive in each succeeding generation. It may be rooted in a particular time and place, but it is somehow ageless and universal. Avoid the current trend or fad. Hold to what is classic.

What is old and familiar does not have to be stale. If it is proclaimed—not just read—with clarity and an emotional honesty, a classic text, no matter what its age, will sound fresh and alive.

WE MARRIED in the early seventies, the era of the lava lamp, and when every wedding included a reading from Gibran's *The Prophet*. You know, "To wake at dawn with a winged heart . . ." Or maybe it had a reading from *The Velveteen Rabbit*. Well, we were going to be different! We asked his aunt to read from a picture book called *The Giving Tree*. She was a children's librarian, and did a great job. Well, we were different. Very unique. But when we remember it now, we groan and crack up.

There are ways of weaving favorite nonscriptural readings into your wedding celebration even if you can't use them as the main readings. Consider these options.

- *Design your own wedding invitation and include a favorite passage as part of the design.*
- *Produce a leaflet that outlines the service so guests unfamiliar with its structure, hymns, or prayers can follow. Use your nonscriptural reading on its front cover or back page as part of the design. (Examples of such leaflets can be found later in this book.)*
- *Incorporate readings into speeches or toasts that are part of the reception.*
- *When you thank your guests at the rehearsal dinner, preface your remarks by reading them something that means a lot to you.*
- *Use a brief passage to toast each other.*

I ATTENDED WHAT felt like the gazillionth wedding of my life. When the groom's father stood to do the reading and said it was from Paul's Letter to the Corinthians, I groaned inside. "Here we go again." But then I was blown away. He delivered the whole passage by heart—not just by rote—it was part of him. It was as if he were speaking directly to his son and his new daughter-in-law, telling them what he personally thought about love and about the power of love. He spoke from his heart, and I heard it as I'd never heard it before.

Structure and Flow

There is a natural rhythm and flow to the way most churches structure this section of the ceremony. It avoids simply piling one reading hard against another, but spaces them in a way that gives the listeners time to appreciate them. The pattern follows the give-and-take of a good conversation—speak, reflect, and respond. The reading is proclaimed. It is followed by a moment of silence. And there is the chance for a response.

An example comes out of the traditional Roman Catholic service: The reader stands, announces the reading with a formal introduction ("A reading from . . ."), proclaims the passage, and concludes it with a formal statement ("The word of the Lord"— to which people respond "Thanks be to God"). The reading is followed by a half-minute to a minute of silence. Then the minister of song leads the congregation in singing a responsorial psalm. The presider then follows with the proclamation of the gospel, using much the same format as for the first reading, and preaches a homily. Then he or she usually sits and gives the assembly more time to meditate in silence.

In informal ceremonies you can be more creative in how you structure this section of the service, but retain that same natural rhythm—reading, silence, response.

Silence

Words lose their power and impact if they are crowded together, one on top of another, without breathing space, without surrounding silence.

If silence occurs naturally and with deliberation during a ceremony, it unites us (we are silent together), it prepares us for what is about to happen, and it gives us time to absorb words or actions that have just occurred. It creates a respectful, open attitude. Silence makes space in our hearts and minds for words to speak in all their power.

A receptive silence prepares the congregation, makes them ready to attend to what is about to happen: to the words that are about to be spoken or to the action about to be performed. You want this sort of silence to precede most significant moments in the ceremony. The minister will often ask the congregation for a moment of silence before praying. An accomplished reader will pause briefly before proclaiming the passage. As a general rule, precede any significant moment in the ceremony with a moment of silence.

A reflective silence gives people time to absorb what they have heard, to think about it, to let their feelings sink in, to catch their breath before moving on to something new. Moments of silence following the presider's reflection (the sermon), a stirring piece of music, or a well-spoken reading are all appropriate.

Language That Welcomes All

For centuries, the English language has favored the masculine noun and pronoun when speaking generally of people. "Man" and "mankind" stood for the entire human race, both sexes. "Men" meant "men and women"; "brothers" meant "brothers and sisters." And "the brotherhood of men" stood in contrast to "man's inhumanity to man." Women were seldom mentioned and, as such, kept invisible. Today such language offends many people—both male and female—who regard it a reflection of the way society has historically denied women's equality and visibility.

As hospitable hosts, you will want to make every effort to avoid needlessly offending any of your guests. Be careful, then, to use language that acknowledges and values everyone. Examine the readings, the prayers, the words you will speak at your ceremony (or in the printed material you prepare). It isn't hard to craft English sentences that adequately and truthfully reflect the totality of our human experience. With a little thought you can say men and women, male and female, humankind, the human race, people, brothers and sisters, he and she or they, as the case may be.

Readings from the Bible, however, pose a special dilemma to sensitive ears. Scripture reflects the biases of two languages—the Hebrew or Greek of the original text and the English of the translation. The New Revised Standard Version of the Bible (NRSV), a translation accepted by many churches for use during worship, is careful to use inclusive language when referring to human beings. The translation we cite in this book, the New Jerusalem Bible, does not adequately address the issue. You might want to consult the NRSV as an alternative or, after consulting your presider, make the changes that are necessary.

We have not changed the texts offered in this book, leaving that to your own discretion.

Readings from Scripture

Old Testament or Hebrew Scriptures

We have included a few sentences of explanation before each reading which your reader might use by way of introduction.

GENESIS 1:26–28, 31A - The first reading tells the story of the world's creation. In it God fashions man and woman on the last day, as the summation and fulfillment of all that has come before. Male and female are—together, not separately—the image and likeness of God. In marriage, the union of a man and woman brings into being a new creation—a new reflection of God.

A reading from the Book of Genesis

> God said,
> "Let us make man in our own image,
> in the likeness of ourselves,
> and let them be masters of the fish of the sea,
> the birds of heaven, the cattle, all the wild animals
> and all the creatures that creep along the ground.
> God created man in the image of himself,
> in the image of God he created him,
> male and female he created them.
> God blessed them, saying to them,
> "Be fruitful and multiply,
> fill the earth and subdue it.
> Be masters of the fish of the sea,
> the birds of heaven and all the living creatures that move on
>   earth."
> God saw all he had made, and indeed it was very good.
> The Word of the Lord.

GENESIS 2:18–24 - In this first reading, taken from the story of the Garden of Eden, God creates woman from the rib of man that the two might be equal. Marriage is the union of man and woman in a love so complete that two become one.

A reading from the Book of Genesis

> Yahweh God said,
> "It is not right that the man should be alone.
> I shall make him a helper."
> So from the soil Yahweh God fashioned all the wild animals

and all the birds of heaven.
These he brought to the man to see what he would call them;
each one was to bear the name the man would give it.
The man gave names to all the cattle,
all the birds of heaven, and all the wild animals.
But no helper suitable for the man was found for him.
Then, Yahweh God made the man fall into a deep sleep.
And, while he was asleep,
he took one of his ribs and closed the flesh up again
forthwith.
Yahweh God fashioned the rib he had taken from the man
into a woman,
and brought her to the man.
And the man said:
"This one at last is bone of my bones and flesh of my flesh!
She is to be called woman, because she was taken from
man."
This is why a man leaves his father and mother
and becomes attached to his wife, and they become one flesh.
The Word of the Lord.

TOBIT 8:5–7 - The first reading, from the Book of Tobit, tells the story of a man's many adventures. He marries a woman who has been previously married seven times and previously widowed seven times on her wedding night. Tobit is saved from the same fate by this prayer which praises God, remembers God's faithfulness, and asks for God's protection.

A reading from the Book of Tobit

You are blessed, O God of our fathers;
blessed too is your name
for ever and ever.
Let the heavens bless you
and all things you have made
for evermore.
You it was who created Adam,
you who created Eve his wife
to be his help and support;
and from these two
the human race was born.
You it was who said,
"It is not right that the man should be alone;
let us make him a helper like him."
And so I take my sister not for any lustful motive,
but I do it in singleness of heart.
Be kind enough to have pity on her and on me
and bring us to old age together.
The Word of the Lord.

SONG OF SONGS 2:8–17 - The Song of Songs is a collection of love songs sung back and forth between two lovers. It celebrates love—even sensuous love—as an embodiment of God's love.

A reading from the Song of Songs

(This selection should be read by a woman)

I hear my love,
See how he comes
leaping on the mountains,
bounding over the hills.
My love is like a gazelle,
like a young stag.
See where he stands
behind our wall.
He looks in at the window,
he peers through the opening.
My love lifts up his voice,
he says to me,
"Come then, my beloved,
my lovely one, come.
For see, winter is past,
the rains are over and gone.
Flowers are appearing on the earth.
The season of glad songs has come,
the cooing of the turtledove is heard in our land.
The fig tree is forming its first figs
and the blossoming vines give out their fragrance.
Come then, my beloved,
my lovely one, come.
My dove, hiding in the clefts of the rock,
in the coverts of the cliff,
show me your face,
let me hear your voice;

for your voice is sweet
and your face is lovely."
My love is mine and I am his.
He pastures his flock among the lilies.
Before the day breeze rises,
before the shadows flee, return!
Be, my love, like a gazelle, like a young stag,
on the mountains of Bether.
The Word of the Lord.

A reading from the Song of Songs

(This can be read by two readers, a woman and a man)

(Female reader)

I hear my love,
See how he comes
leaping on the mountains,
bounding over the hills.
My love is like a gazelle,
like a young stag.
See where he stands
behind our wall.
He looks in at the window,
he peers through the opening.
My love lifts up his voice,
he says to me,

(Male reader)

"Come then, my beloved,
my lovely one, come.

For see, winter is past,

the rains are over and gone.

Flowers are appearing on the earth.

The season of glad songs has come,

the cooing of the turtledove is heard in our land.

The fig tree is forming its first figs

and the blossoming vines give out their fragrance.

Come then, my beloved,

my lovely one, come.

My dove, hiding in the clefts of the rock,

in the coverts of the cliff,

show me your face,

let me hear your voice;

for your voice is sweet

and your face is lovely."

(Female reader)

My love is mine and I am his.

He pastures his flock among the lilies.

Before the day breeze rises,

before the shadows flee, return!

Be, my love, like a gazelle, like a young stag,

on the mountains of Bether.

The Word of the Lord.

ISAIAH 61:10–11 - The prophet Isaiah celebrates God's power in leading the exiled people of Israel out of captivity back to the promised land. He likens his joy to the joy of a bride and groom. So, too, may the joy of married couples reflect the saving power of God.

A reading from the Book of the prophet Isaiah

> *I exult for joy in Yahweh,*
> *my soul rejoices in my God,*
> *for he has clothed me in garments of salvation,*
> *he has wrapped me in a cloak of saving justice,*
> *like a bridegroom wearing his garland,*
> *like a bride adorned in her jewels.*
> *For as the earth sends up its shoots*
> *and a garden makes seeds sprout,*
> *so Lord Yahweh makes saving justice and praise*
> *spring up in the sight of all nations.*
> *The Word of the Lord.*

JEREMIAH 31:31–32A, 33–34A - The prophet Jeremiah speaks to a people defeated in battle and oppressed by poverty, and he consoles them with God's promise of a new covenant. A covenant, more than a contract, signifies a deep union of heart and mind, a union that finds its deepest realization in marriage.

A reading from the Book of the prophet Jeremiah

> *Look, the days are coming, Yahweh declares,*
> *when I shall make a new covenant with the House of Israel,*
> *but not like the covenant I made with their ancestors*
> *the day I took them by the hand to bring them out of Egypt.*
> *No, this is the covenant I shall make with the House of*
>   *Israel*
> *when those days have come, Yahweh declares.*
> *Within them I shall place my Law, writing it on their hearts.*

Then I shall be their God and they will be my people.
There will be no further need for everyone to teach neighbor
or brother,
saying, "Learn to know Yahweh."
No, they will all know me, from the least to the greatest.
The Word of the Lord.

HOSEA 2:16–21 - The prophet Hosea taught that God's relationship with the chosen people was most fully symbolized by the marriage between a man and a woman.

A reading from the Book of the prophet Hosea

But look, I am going to seduce her
and lead her into the desert
and speak to her heart.
There I shall give her back her vineyards
and make the Vale of Achor a gateway of hope.
There she will respond
    as when she was young,
as on the day when she came up from Egypt.
When that day comes
    —declares Yahweh—
you will call me, "My husband."

When that day comes
I shall make a treaty for them with the wild animals,
with the birds of heaven
and the creeping things of the earth;
I shall break the bow and the sword

and warfare, and banish them from the country,
and I will let them sleep secure.
I shall betroth you to myself for ever,
I shall betroth you
in uprightness and justice
and faithful love and tenderness.
The Word of the Lord.

Hosea 2:16–21 (NEB)

I will woo her,
I will go with her into the wilderness and comfort her:
there I will restore her vineyards,
turning the Vale of Trouble into the Gate of Hope,
and there she will answer as in her youth,
when she came up out of Egypt.
On that day she shall call me, "My husband."
Then I will make a covenant on behalf of Israel with the
    wild beasts,
the birds of the air,
and the things that creep on the earth,
and I will break bow and sword and weapon of war
and sweep them off the earth,
so that all living creatures may lie down without fear.
I will betroth you to myself forever,
betroth you in lawful wedlock
with unfailing devotion and love;
I will betroth you to myself to have and to hold, . . .
The Word of the Lord.

Epistle Readings

ROMANS 8:31B–35, 37–39 - In his letter to the church at Rome, the apostle Paul proclaims the indomitable power of God's love—a love that overcomes all separation. Married love, a reflection of God's love, shares in its power to bridge all divisions.

A reading from Paul's Letter to the Romans

> *If God is for us, who can be against us?*
> *Since he did not spare his own Son,*
> *but gave him up for the sake of all of us,*
> *then can we not expect that with him he will freely give us*
>   *all his gifts?*
> *Who can bring any accusation against those that God has*
>   *chosen?*
> *When God grants saving justice who can condemn?*
> *Are we not sure that it is Christ Jesus, who died*
> *—yes, and more, who was raised from the dead and is at*
>   *God's right hand—*
> *and who is adding his pleas for us?*
> *Can anything cut us off from the love of Christ*
> *—can hardship or distress or persecution,*
> *or lack of food and clothing, or threats or violence.*
> *No; we come through all these things triumphantly victorious,*
> *by the power of him who loved us.*
> *For I am certain of this:*
> *neither death nor life, nor angels, nor principalities,*
> *nothing already in existence and nothing still to come,*
> *nor any power, nor the heights nor the depths,*

nor any created thing whatever,
will be able to come between us and the love of God,
known to us in Christ Jesus our Lord.
The word of the Lord.

ROMANS 12:9–18 - In his letter to the church at Rome, the apostle Paul describes the sort of love that undergirds and upholds any lasting marriage—a love based on joy, perseverance, prayers, charity, and hospitality.

A reading from Paul's Letter to the Romans

Let love be without any pretense.
Avoid what is evil;
stick to what is good.
In love let your feelings of deep affection for one another come
*   to expression*
and regard others as more important than yourself.
In the service of the Lord,
work not halfheartedly but with conscientiousness and an
*   eager spirit.*
Be joyful in hope,
persevere in hardship;
keep praying regularly;
share with any of God's holy people who are in need;
look for opportunities to be hospitable.
Bless your persecutors; never curse them, bless them.
Rejoice with others when they rejoice, and be sad with those
*   in sorrow.*
Give the same consideration to all others alike.

Pay no regard to social standing,
but meet humble people on their own terms.
Do not congratulate yourself on your own wisdom.
Never pay back evil with evil,
but bear in mind the ideal that all regard with respect.
As much as possible, and to the utmost of your ability,
be at peace with everyone.
The word of the Lord.

ROMANS 13:8–10 - In his letter to the church at Rome, the apostle Paul proclaimed the centrality of love in the life of Christians.

A reading from Paul's Letter to the Romans

The only thing you should owe to anyone is love for one
another,
for to love the other person is to fulfill the law.
All these:
You shall not commit adultery,
You shall not kill,
You shall not steal,
You shall not covet,
and all the other commandments that there are, are
summed up
in this single phrase:
You must love your neighbor as yourself.
Love can cause no harm to your neighbor,
and to love is the fulfillment of the law.
The word of the Lord.

(To cut down the length of this reading, you might want to consider omitting the sections in brackets.)

I CORINTHIANS 12:31–13:1–13 - In Paul's great hymn of love, he describes the attitudes and the habits of the heart that love makes possible and that, in turn, make love possible.

A reading from Paul's First Letter to the Corinthians

> *[Set your mind on the higher gifts.*
> *And now I am going to put before you the best way of all.*
> *Though I command languages both human and angelic*
> *—if I speak without love,*
> *I am no more than a gong booming or a cymbal clashing.*
> *And though I have the power of prophecy,*
> *to penetrate all mysteries and knowledge,*
> *and though I have all the faith necessary to move mountains*
> *—if I am without love, I am nothing.*
> *Though I should give away to the poor all that I possess,*
> *and even give up my body to be burned*
> *—if I am without love,*
> *it will do me no good whatever.]*
> *Love is always patient and kind;*
> *love is never jealous;*
> *love is not boastful or conceited,*
> *it is never rude and never seeks its own advantage,*
> *it does not take offense or store up grievances.*
> *Love does not rejoice at wrongdoing,*
> *but finds its joy in the truth.*
> *It is always ready to make allowances,*

to trust,

to hope

and to endure whatever comes.

Love never comes to an end.

[But if there are prophecies,

they will be done away with;

if tongues, they will fall silent;

and if knowledge, it will be done away with.

For we know only imperfectly,

and we prophesy imperfectly;

but once perfection comes,

all imperfect things will be done away with.]

When I was a child,

I used to talk like a child,

and see things as a child does,

and think like a child;

but now that I have become an adult,

I have finished with all childish ways.

Now we see only reflections in a mirror, mere riddles,

but then we shall be seeing face to face.

Now I can know only imperfectly;

but then I shall know just as fully as I am myself known.

As it is, these remain: faith, hope, and love,

the three of them;

and the greatest of them is love.

The word of the Lord.

EPHESIANS 3:14–20 - In the Letter to the Ephesians, the apostle Paul prays for all believers a prayer suited for a couple beginning a new life together—a life planted in love and built on love.

A reading from Paul's Letter to the Ephesians

> *This, then, is what I pray, kneeling before the Father,*
> *from whom every fatherhood, in heaven or on earth, takes its*
> *   name.*
> *In the abundance of his glory*
> *may God, through his Spirit, enable you to grow firm*
> *in power with regard to your inner self,*
> *so that Christ may live in your hearts through faith,*
> *and then, planted in love and built on love,*
> *with all God's holy people*
> *you will have the strength to grasp*
> *the breadth and the length,*
> *the height and the depth:*
> *so that, knowing the love of Christ, which is beyond*
> *   knowledge,*
> *you may be filled with the utter fullness of God.*
> *Glory be to him whose power, working in us,*
> *can do infinitely more than we can ask or imagine;*
> *glory be to him from generation to generation*
> *in the Church and in Christ Jesus for ever and ever.* Amen.
> *The word of the Lord.*

COLOSSIANS 3:12–17 - In the Letter to the Colossians, the apostle Paul describes the love which is a foundation to any lasting marriage—a love based on compassion, generosity, gentleness, forgiveness, and gratitude.

A reading from Paul's Letter to the Colossians

> As the chosen of God, then,
> the holy people whom he loves,
> you are to be clothed in heartfelt compassion,
> in generosity and humility, gentleness and patience.
> Bear with one another;
> forgive each other if one of you has a complaint against
>   another.
> The Lord has forgiven you; now you must do the same.
> Over all these clothes, put on love, the perfect bond.
> And may the peace of Christ reign in your hearts,
> because it is for this that you were called together in one body.
> Always be thankful.
> Let the Word of Christ, in all its richness, find a home with
>   you.
> Teach each other, and advise each other, in all wisdom.
> With gratitude in your hearts
> sing psalms and hymns and inspired songs to God;
> and whatever you say or do, let it be in the name of the Lord
>   Jesus,
> in thanksgiving to God the Father through him.
> The word of the Lord.

1 JOHN 3:18–24 - The apostle John describes a quality of love—active and genuine—which also fortifies a lasting marriage.

A reading from the First Letter of John

> *Children, our love must be not just words or mere talk,*
> *but something active and genuine.*
> *This will be the proof that we belong to the truth,*
> *and it will convince us in his presence,*
> *even if your own feelings condemn us,*
> *that God is greater than our feelings and knows all things.*
> *My dear friends, if our own feelings do not condemn us,*
> *we can be fearless before God,*
> *and whatever we ask we shall receive from him,*
> *because we keep his commandment and do what is acceptable*
> *   to him.*
> *His command is this,*
> *that we should believe in the name of his Son Jesus Christ*
> *and that we should love one another as he commanded us.*
> *Whoever keeps his commandments remains in God, and God*
> *   in him.*
> *And this is the proof that he remains in us:*
> *the Spirit that he has given us.*
> *The word of the Lord.*

I JOHN 4:7–12 - The apostle John describes the mystery of love: God is love! Marriage, then, is more than a couple's love for each other: It is, at the same time, the love of God made visible.

A reading from the First Letter of John

> *My dear friends, let us love one another,*
> *since love is from God*

and everyone who loves is a child of God and knows God.
Whoever fails to love does not know God, because God is
   love.
This is the revelation of God's love for us,
that God sent his only Son into the world
that we might have life through him.
Love consists in this:
it is not we who loved God,
but God loved us and sent his Son to expiate our sins.
My dear friends,
if God loves us so much, we too should love one another.
No one has ever seen God,
but as long as we love one another God remains in us
and his love comes to its perfection in us.
The word of the Lord.

Gospel Readings

MATTHEW 5:1–12 – In the Sermon on the Mount, Jesus announced his vision of a new creation—what he called the reign of God. In his vision, those who rely on God and act with justice and mercy are blessed. A marriage, founded on love, is also blessed.

A reading from the Gospel according to Matthew

   Seeing the crowds, he went onto the mountain.
   And when he was seated his disciples came to him.
   Then he began to speak.
   This is what he taught them:

How blessed are the poor in spirit:
the kingdom of Heaven is theirs.
Blessed are the gentle:
they shall have the earth as inheritance.
Blessed are those who mourn:
they shall be comforted.
Blessed are those who hunger and thirst for uprightness:
they shall have their fill.
Blessed are the merciful:
they shall have mercy shown them.
Blessed are the pure in heart:
they shall see God.
Blessed are the peacemakers:
they shall be recognized as children of God.
Blessed are those who are persecuted in the cause of
   uprightness:
the kingdom of Heaven is theirs.
Blessed are you when people abuse you and persecute you
and speak all kinds of calumny against you falsely on my ac-
count.
Rejoice and be glad, for your reward will be great in heaven;
this is how they persecuted the prophets before you.
The gospel of the Lord.

MATTHEW 5:13–16 - In the Sermon on the Mount, Jesus de-
scribed his vision of a new creation—what he called the reign of
God. In his vision, those who follow him add flavor and taste to
what is bland and cast light on an otherwise dreary world. In
marriage two followers of Jesus add their own spice and illumi-
nation, as they work toward the reign of God.

A reading from the Gospel according to Matthew

> You are salt for the earth.
> But if salt loses its taste,
> what can make it salty again?
> It is good for nothing, and can only be thrown out
> to be trampled under people's feet.
> You are light for the world.
> A city built on a hill-top cannot be hidden.
> No one lights a lamp to put it under a tub,
> they put it on the lamp-stand where it shines for everyone in
>   the house.
> In the same way your light must shine in people's sight,
> so that, seeing your good works,
> they may give praise to your Father in heaven.
> The gospel of the Lord.

MATTHEW 6:25–34 - Under God's care and protection, there is no need for anxiety or grasping. At the beginning of a marriage, especially in these anxious times, it is good to remember what truly matters.

A reading from the Gospel according to Matthew

> That is why I am telling you not to worry about your life
> and what you are to eat,
> nor about your body and what you are to wear.
> Surely life is more than food, and the body more than
>   clothing!
> Look at the birds in the sky.

They do not sow or reap or gather into barns;

yet your heavenly Father feeds them.

Are you not worth much more than they are?

Can any of you, however much you worry,

add one single cubit to your span of life?

And why worry about clothing?

Think of the flowers growing in the fields;

they never have to work or spin;

yet I assure you that not even Solomon in all his royal robes

was clothed like one of these.

Now if that is how God clothes the wild flowers growing in
  the field

which are there today and thrown into the furnace tomorrow,

will he not much more look about you,

you who have so little faith?

So do not worry; do not say,

"What are we to eat? What are we to drink? What are we
  to wear?"

It is the gentiles who set their hearts on all these things.

Your heavenly Father knows you need them all.

Set your hearts on his kingdom first,

and on God's saving justice,

and all these other things will be given you as well.

So do not worry about tomorrow;

tomorrow will take care of itself.

Each day has enough trouble of its own.

The gospel of the Lord.

MARK 6:34–44 - Jesus frequently compared the reign of God
to a banquet—often to a wedding banquet—where the hungry

are fed and all sorrow gives way to dancing. At the beginning of a marriage, especially in these anxious times, it is good to remember God's bounty and care for us.

A reading from the Gospel according to Mark

> As he stepped ashore he saw a large crowd;
> and he took pity on them
> because they were like sheep without a shepherd,
> and he set himself to teach them at some length.
> By now it was getting very late
> and his disciples came up to him and said,
> "This is a lonely place and it is getting very late,
> so send them away,
> and they can go to the farms and villages round about,
> to buy themselves something to eat."
> He replied, "Give them something to eat yourselves."
> They answered,
> "Are we to go and spend two hundred denari on bread for
>   them to eat?"
> He asked, "How many loaves have you? Go and see."
> And when they had found out they said, "Five, and two
>   fish."
> Then he ordered them to get all the people
> to sit down in groups on the green grass,
> and they sat down on the ground in squares of hundreds and
>   fifties.
> Then he took the five loaves and the two fish,
> raised his eyes to heaven and said the blessing;
> then he broke the loaves

and began handing them to his disciples to distribute among
    the people.
He also shared out the two fish among them all.
They all ate as much as they wanted.
They collected twelve basketfuls of scraps of bread and pieces
    of fish.
Those who had eaten the loaves numbered five thousand
    men.
The gospel of the Lord.

MARK 10:6–9 - In this Gospel reading, Jesus recalls God's will from the beginning of all time—that the union of a man and woman be so complete that it cannot be divided.

A reading from the Gospel according to Mark

From the beginning of creation
he made them male and female.
This is why a man leaves his father and mother,
and the two become one flesh.
They are no longer two, therefore, but one flesh.
So then, what God has united, human beings must not
    divide.
The gospel of the Lord.

MARK 12:28–31 - In this Gospel reading, Jesus sums up all the five hundred and twelve commandments of the Law in just two—the love of God and the love of neighbor.

A reading from the Gospel according to Mark

> *One of the scribes who had listened to them debating*
> *appreciated that Jesus had given a good answer*
> *and put a further question to him,*
> *"Which is the first of all the commandments?"*
> *Jesus replied, "This is the first:*
> *Listen, Israel, the Lord our God is the one, only Lord,*
> *and you must love the Lord your God*
> *with all your heart, with all your soul, with all your mind,*
> *and with all your strength.*
> *The second is this:*
> *You must love your neighbor as yourself.*
> *There is no commandment greater than these."*
> *The gospel of the Lord.*

JOHN 2:1–11 - In today's Gospel reading, Jesus attends a wedding feast as a guest. He blesses it by turning water into wine. When we live with love, we, too, can turn the ordinary into the extraordinary.

A reading from the Gospel according to John

> *On the third day, there was a wedding at Cana in Galilee.*
> *The mother of Jesus was there,*
> *and Jesus and his disciples had also been invited.*
> *And they ran out of wine,*
> *since the wine provided for the feast had all been used,*
> *and the mother of Jesus said to him, "They have no wine."*

Jesus said, "Woman, what do you want from me?
My hour has not come yet."
His mother said to the servants, "Do whatever he tells you."
There were six stone water jars standing there,
meant for the ablutions that are customary among the Jews:
each could hold twenty or thirty gallons.
Jesus said to the servants, "Fill the jars with water,"
and they filled them to the brim.
Then he said to them,
"Draw some out now and take it to the president of the
  feast."
They did this; the president tasted the water,
and it had turned into wine.
Having no idea where it came from
—though the servants who had drawn the water knew—
the president of the feast called the bridegroom and said,
"Everyone serves good wine first
and the worse wine when the guests are well wined;
but you have kept the best wine till now."
The gospel of the Lord.

JOHN 13:4–15 - In this Gospel reading, Jesus gives an example of the self-sacrificing love which is necessary to sustain a marriage.

A reading from the Gospel according to John

Jesus got up from the table,
removed his outer garments and,

taking a towel, wrapped it round his waist;

he then poured water into a basin and began to wash the
disciples' feet

and to wipe them with the towel he was wearing.

He came to Simon Peter, who said to him,

"Lord, are you going to wash my feet?"

Jesus answered, "At the moment you do not know what I
am doing,

but later you will understand."

"Never!" said Peter. "You shall never wash my feet."

Jesus replied, "If I do not wash you, you can have no share
with me."

Simon Peter said, "Well then, Lord, not only my feet,

but my hands and my head as well!"

Jesus said, "No one who has had a bath needs washing,

such a person is clean all over.

You too are clean, though not all of you are."

He knew who was going to betray him,

and that was why he said, "though not all of you are."

When he had washed their feet and put on his outer
garments again

he went back to the table.

"Do you understand," he said, "what I have done to you?

You call me Master and Lord, and rightly; so I am.

If I, then, the Lord and Master, have washed your feet,

you must wash each other's feet.

I have given you an example,

so that you may copy what I have done to you."

The gospel of the Lord.

JOHN 15:9–12 - Jesus reminds his followers of his love for them, a love we are invited to continue by sharing it with each other.

A reading from the Gospel according to John

> *I have loved you just as the Father has loved me.*
> *Remain in my love.*
> *If you keep my commandments, you will remain in my love,*
> *just as I have kept my Father's commandments and remain in*
> *his love.*
> *I have told you this so that my own joy may be in you*
> *and your joy be complete.*
> *This is my commandment: love one another, as I have loved*
> *you.*
> *The gospel of the Lord.*

JOHN 15:12–16 - Jesus commands his followers to love others as he has loved them and to follow his example of laying down his life for others. Unselfish love is at the heart of a true marriage.

A reading from the Gospel according to John

> *This is my commandment:*
> *love one another, as I have loved you.*
> *No one can have greater love than to lay down his life for his*
> *friends.*
> *You are my friends, if you do what I command you.*
> *I shall no longer call you servants,*

because a servant does not know the master's business;
I call you friends, because I have made known to you
  everything
I have learnt from my Father.
You did not choose me, no, I chose you;
and I commissioned you to go out and to bear fruit,
fruit that will last;
so that the Father will give you anything you ask him in my
  name.
The gospel of the Lord.

Readings from Literature

Sonnet XVII
Pablo Neruda

I don't love you as if you were the salt-rose, topaz
or arrow of carnations that propagate fire:
I love you as certain dark things are loved,
secretly, between the shadow and the soul.

I love you as the plant that doesn't bloom and carries
hidden within itself the light of those flowers,

and thanks to your love, darkly in my body
lives the dense fragrance that rises from the earth.

I love you without knowing how, or when, or from where,
I love you simply, without problems or pride:
I love you in this way because I don't know another way of
*   loving.*

but this, in which there is no I or you,
so intimate that your hand upon my chest is my hand,
so intimate that when I fall asleep it is your eyes that close.

THE LOVE OF GOD
Dante

The love of God, unutterable and perfect,
flows into a pure soul the way that light
rushes into a transparent object.
The more love that it finds, the more it gives
itself, so that, as we grow clear and open,
the more complete the joy of loving is.
And the more souls who resonate together,
the greater the intensity of their love,
for, mirror-like, each soul reflects the other.

FROM ROMEO AND JULIET

William Shakespeare

Juliet: *Good-night, good-night! as sweet repose and rest*
           Come to thy heart as that within my breast!

Romeo: *O! wilt thou leave me so unsatisfied?*

Juliet: *What satisfaction canst thou have tonight?*

Romeo: *The exchange of thy love's faithful vow for mine.*

Juliet: *I gave thee mine before thou didst request it;*
           And yet I would it were to give again.

Romeo: *Wouldst thou withdraw it? for what purpose, love?*

Juliet: *But to be frank, and give it thee again.*
           And yet I wish but for the thing I have:
           My bounty is as boundless as the sea,
           My love as deep; the more I give to thee,
           The more I have, both are infinite.

SONNET 116

William Shakespeare

Let me not to the marriage of true minds
Admit impediments; love is not love
Which alters when it alteration finds
Or bends with the remover to remove
O no, it is an ever-fixed mark
That looks on the tempests and is never shaken,
It is the star to every wand'ring bark,
Whose worth's unknown, although his height be taken
Love's not Time's fool, though rosy lips and cheeks

Within his bending sickle's compass come,
Love alters not with his brief hours and weeks,
But bears it out even to the edge of doom
  If this be error and upon me proved
  I never writ, nor no man ever loved.

FROM *POETRY AND MARRIAGE*
Wendell Berry

The meaning of marriage begins in the giving of words. We cannot join ourselves to one another without giving our word. And this must be an unconditional giving, for in joining ourselves to one another we join ourselves to the unknown. We can join one another *only* by joining the unknown. We must not be misled by the procedures of experimental thought: in life, in the world, we are never given two known results to choose between, but only *one* result: that we choose without knowing what it is . . .

Because the condition of marriage is worldly and its meaning communal, no one party to it can be solely in charge. What you alone think it ought to be, it is not going to be. Where you alone think you want it to go, it is not going to go. It is going where the two of you—and marriage, time, life, history and the world—will take it. You do not know the road; you have committed your life to a way.

GIVE ALL IN LOVE

Ralph Waldo Emerson

Give all in love;
Obey thy heart;
Friends, kindred, days,
Estate, good-fame,
Plans, credit, and the Muse,
Nothing refuse.

'Tis a brave master;
Let it have scope:
Follow it utterly,
Hope beyond hope:
High and more high
It dives into noon,
With wing unspent,
Untold intent;
But it is a god,
Knows its own path
And the outlets of the sky.

It was never for the mean;
It requireth courage stout.
Souls above doubt,
Valor unbending.
It will reward,
They shall return
More than they were,
And ever ascending. . . .

BENEDICTION
Stanley Kunitz

God banish from your house
The fly, the roach, the mouse
That riots in the walls
Until the plaster falls;
Admonish from your door
The hypocrite and liar;
No shy, soft, tigrish fear
Permit upon your stair,
Nor agents of your doubt.
God drive them whistling out.

Let nothing touched with evil,
Let nothing that can shrivel
Heart's tenderest frond, intrude
Upon your still, deep blood.
Against the drip of night
God keep all windows tight,
Protect your mirrors from
Surprise, delirium,
Admit no trailing wind
Into your shuttered mind
To plume the lake of sleep
With dreams. If you must weep
God give you tears, but leave
You secrecy to grieve,
And islands for your pride,
And love to nest in your side.

THE COUNTRY OF MARRIAGE
Wendell Berry

. . . *our life reminds me*
of a forest in which there is a graceful clearing
and in that opening a house,
an orchard and garden,
comfortable shades, and flowers . . .
The forest is mostly dark, its ways
to be made anew day after day, the dark
richer than the light and more blessed,
provided we stay brave
enough to keep going in . . .

ONE HUNDRED POEMS FROM THE JAPANESE
Kenneth Rexroth

I have always known
That at last I would
Take this road, but yesterday
I did not know that it would be today

FROM THE CANTOS
Ezra Pound

What thou lov'st well remains,
the rest is dross
What thou lov'st well shall not be

reft from thee
What thou lov'st well is thy true
heritage. . . .

FROM *THE BOOK AND THE BROTHERHOOD*
Iris Murdoch

I hereby give myself. I love you. You are the only being whom
I can love absolutely with my complete self, with all my flesh and
mind and heart. You are my mate, my perfect partner, and I am
yours. You must feel this now, as I do. . . . It was a marvel that
we ever met. It is some kind of divine luck that we are together
now. We must never, never part again. We are, here in this, necessary beings, like gods. As we look at each other we verify, we
know, the perfection of our love, we recognize each other. Here
is my life, here if need be is my death.

MY TRUE LOVE HATH MY HEART
Sir Philip Sidney

My true love hath my heart and I have his,
By just exchange one for another given;
I hold his dear and mine he cannot miss;
There never was a better bargain driven:
My true love hath my heart and I have his.

My heart in me keeps him and me in one;
My heart in him his thoughts and senses guides;
He loves my heart for once it was his own;

I cherish his because in me it bides:
My true love hath my heart and I have his.

From *Letters to a Young Poet*
Rainer Maria Rilke

For one human being to love another human being, that is perhaps the most difficult task that has been entrusted to us, the ultimate task, the final test and proof, the work for which all other work is but preparation . . . [Love] is a high inducement for the individual to ripen . . . to become world in himself for the sake of another person . . . human love . . . consists in this: that two solitudes protect and border and greet each other.

. . . once the realization is accepted that even between the closest human beings infinite distances continue to exist, a wonderful living side by side can grow up, if they succeed in loving the distance between them which makes it possible for each to see the other whole against a wide sky!

From *Adam Bede*
George Eliot

What greater thing is there for two human souls than to feel that they are joined for life, to strengthen each other in all labor, to rest on each other in all sorrow, to minister to each other in all pain, to be one with each other in silent unspeakable memories at the moment of the last parting?

FROM *TO HAVE OR TO BE?*
Erich Fromm

Can one have love? If we could, love would need to be a thing, a substance that one can have, own, possess. The truth is, there is no such thing as "love." "Love" is an abstraction, perhaps a goddess or an alien being, although nobody has ever seen this goddess. In reality, there exists only the act of loving. To love is a productive activity. It implies caring for, knowing, responding, affirming, enjoying: the person, the tree, the painting, the idea. It means bringing to life, increasing his/her/its aliveness. It is a process, self-renewing and self-increasing . . .

To say "I have a great love for you" is meaningless. Love is not a thing that one can have, but a process, an inner activity that one is the subject of, I can love, I can be in love, but in love I *have* . . . nothing. In fact, the less I have, the more I can love.

FROM *GIFT FROM THE SEA*
Anne Morrow Lindbergh

When you love someone you do not love them all the time, in exactly the same way, from moment to moment. It is an impossibility. It is even a lie to pretend to. And yet this is exactly what most of us demand. We have so little faith in the ebb and flow of life, of love, of relationships. We leap at the flow of the tide and resist in terror its ebb. We are afraid it will never return. We insist on permanency, on duration, on continuity; when the only continuity possible, in life as in love, is in growth, in fluidity—in freedom in the sense that the dancers are free, barely touching as they pass, but partners in the same pattern.

Theodore Parker

It takes years to marry completely two hearts, even of the most loving and well assorted. A happy wedlock is a long falling in love. Young persons think love belongs only to the brown-haired and crimson-cheeked. So it does for its beginning. But the golden marriage is a part of love which the Bridal day knows nothing of . . .

Such a large and sweet fruit is a complete marriage that it needs a long summer to ripen in, and then a long winter to mellow and season it. But a really happy marriage of love and judgment between a noble man and woman is one of the things so very handsome that if the sun were, as the Greek poets fabled, a God he might stop the world and hold it still now and then in order to look all day long on some example thereof, and feast his eyes on such a spectacle.

RABBI BEN EZRA
Robert Browning

Grow old along with me!
The best is yet to be,
The last of life, for which the first was made.

THE BAIT
John Donne

Come live with me and be my love,
And we will some new pleasures prove,
Of golden sands and crystal brooks,
With silken lines and silver hoods.

Goethe

It is the true season
of Love
when we know that
we alone can love;
that no one could ever
have loved before us
and that no one
will ever Love
in the same way
after us.

Walt Whitman

I do not offer the old smooth prizes,
But offer rough new prizes,
These are the days that must happen to you:
You shall not heap up what is called riches,
You shall scatter with lavish hands all that you earn or
    achieve.
However sweet the laid-up stores,

However convenient the dwellings,
You shall not remain there.
However sheltered the port,
And however calm the waters,
You shall not anchor there.
However welcome the hospitality that welcomes you
You are permitted to receive it but a little while
Afoot and lighthearted, take to the open road,
Healthy, free, the world before you,
The long brown path before you, leading wherever you
*   choose.*
Say only to one another:
Camerado, I give you my hand!
I give you my love, more precious than money,
I give you myself before preaching or law:
Will you give me yourself?
Will you come travel with me?
Shall we stick by each other as long as we live?

FROM *THE BROTHERS KARAMAZOV*
Fyodor Dostoevsky

Active love is a harsh and fearful thing compared with love in dreams. Love in dreams thirsts for immediate action, quickly performed, and with everyone watching. Indeed, it will go as far as the giving even of one's life, provided it does not take long but is soon over, as on stage, and everyone is looking on and praising. Whereas active love is labor and perseverance, and for some people, perhaps, a whole science. But I predict that even in that very moment when you see with horror that despite all your efforts, you not only have not come nearer your goal but seem to have gotten farther from it, at that very moment—I predict this to you—you will suddenly reach your goal and will clearly behold over you the wonder-working power of the Lord, who all the while has been loving you, and all the while has been mysteriously guiding you.

Shorter Quotations

There is no remedy for love than to love more.   *Henry David Thoreau*

Love is the joy of the good, the wonder of the wise, the amazement of the Gods.   *Plato*

One word frees us all of the weight and pain of life; that word is love.   *Sophocles*

The only gift is a portion of thyself.   *Ralph Waldo Emerson*

Love does not consist in gazing at each other, but in looking outward in the same direction.   *Antoine de Saint-Exupéry*

If there is such a thing as a good marriage, it is because it resembles friendship rather than love.   *Michel de Montaigne*

The minute I heard my first love story I started looking for you, not knowing how blind that was. Lovers don't finally meet somewhere. They're in each other all along.   *Rumi, "The Ruins of the Heart"*

In a time when nothing is more certain than change, the commitment of two people to one another has become difficult and rare. Yet, by its scarcity, the beauty and value of this exchange have only been enhanced.   *Robert Sexton, "The Vow"*

The web of marriage is made by propinquity, in the day-to-day living side by side, looking outward and working outward in the same direction. It is woven in space and in time of the substance of life itself.   *Anne Morrow Lindbergh,* Gift from the Sea

From every human being there rises a light that reaches straight to heaven. And when two souls that are destined to be together find each other, their streams of light flow together, and a single brighter light goes forth from their united being.   *Baal Shem Tov*

Love alone is capable of uniting living beings in such a way as to complete and fulfill them, for it alone takes them and joins them by what is deepest in themselves.   *Pierre Teilhard de Chardin*

There is no necessary relation between love and children, but there is a necessary relation between love and creation. The aim of conscious love is to bring about rebirth.   *A. R. Orange*

To find the soul one must step back from the surface, go deep within, and center, enter . . . and then there is something warm, tranquil, rich, very still, and very full, like a sweetness—this is soul.   *Sri Aurobindo*

What now seems to you opaque, you will make transparent with your blazing heart.   *Rainer Maria Rilke*

Giving Consent and Exchanging Vows

The heart of the wedding ceremony and its high point is the exchange of vows. In the presence of the minister or priest and of your families and friends, you say the words that only begin to express your intent. In what must surely be one of life's most daring acts you say, in effect, "I give you myself, all that I am and may become, holding nothing back. I bind myself to you in love now and forever, without condition or reservation."

Vows have an ancient, almost primal religious sense about them. The contemporary definition has changed little from its original meaning—a vow is a solemn pledge a person makes to God to perform an act or to make a sacrifice in return for a favor.

In the Hebrew Scriptures, when people were in distress or under attack, they begged God for help—as we still do when we're in trouble—and made a vow. In return for God's assistance, they promised to make a sacrifice, to offer a lamb, or a goat, or if they were truly poor, a pair of doves. The Hebrew word *neber* means both vow and sacrifice.

The Jewish practice and concept of making vows to God carried over into Christianity, although in a changed form since Christians no longer offered animals in sacrifice. Instead, they offered themselves. They offered whatever was of value to them— their possessions, their time, their service, their devotion—to God in return for the favor God had already granted them, the favor of redemption. Some Christians made private vows, promising perhaps to go on pilgrimage to a nearby shrine, while others made formal, public vows, promising, for example, to lead a life of poverty.

A vow is made to God. It is made in return for a favor or a blessing, and it commits the person making it to perform a sacrifice.

The wedding vow most couples exchange today reaches through the centuries. Its current form is "I take you for my lawful husband/wife, to have and to hold, from this day forward, for better, for worse, for richer, for poorer, in sickness and in health, until death do us part." In almost every respect it deviates from the customary format of a vow. It is spoken not to God but to another person. It asks for no favor or blessing in return. And it makes no mention of offering sacrifice.

Give it some thought, however, and the wedding promise does incorporate all three aspects of a vow.

You are making a solemn promise to God. First, God is in and with your beloved. Not to say that your beloved *is* God but that God is within everything as its breath and animating spirit. Christians believe that through baptism the Spirit of God dwells within each believer. It is the vocation of each married couple to find how their love for each other complements and fulfills their love for God and God's love for them. God is also present in the community that hears you speak your vows. You began your ceremony by invoking God's name and asking that Christ be present. Christ promised, "Wherever two or three are gathered in my name, there I am in their midst."

You make your vows both in response to a blessing and in anticipation of one. The blessing? The person who has loved you and now promises to love you forever.

Finally, you commit yourself to making a sacrifice. The love you pledge to each other—for better or for worse—will demand, perhaps, many sacrifices of you. At times in your marriage you will need to forgo your own wishes and preferences, the demands of your ego, your self-sufficiency, your freedom. Each time you choose to love when it would be easier or more convenient to look after your own interests, you make a sacrifice. You take some part of yourself and give it to God, trusting that God will accept your sacrifice and bless it in return.

In a more all-embracing way, you choose to make your entire life together a sacrifice. The word comes from the Latin, *sacra* meaning "holy" and *facere* meaning "to make." If you do indeed share your love without reservation, or condition, or any guarantee of what the future may hold, if you support, nurture, cherish, and comfort each other through all the vicissitudes of life, and if you are open to the possibility of having children and of providing for them and their welfare, you are indeed "making holy"

your life. This sort of sacrifice is what a character from Dosto-
evsky's novel *The Brothers Karamazov* calls a "whole science":

> Active love is a harsh and fearful thing compared with love
> in dreams. Love in dreams thirsts for immediate action,
> quickly performed, and with everyone watching. Indeed, it
> will go as far as the giving even of one's life, provided it
> does not take long but is soon over, as on stage, and every-
> one is looking on and praising. Whereas active love is labor
> and perseverance, and for some people, perhaps, a whole
> science. But I predict that even in that very moment when
> you see with horror that despite all your efforts, you not
> only have not come nearer your goal but seem to have got-
> ten farther from it, at that very moment—I predict this to
> you—you will suddenly reach your goal and will clearly
> behold over you the wonder-working power of the Lord,
> who all the while has been loving you, and all the while has
> been mysteriously guiding you.

The Couple's Declaration of Consent

The exchange of vows is a momentous undertaking, one that
should not be assumed lightly or without reflection. Before you
recite your vows to each other, the presider will ask you to state
your intentions. He or she will ask you a question or, possibly, a
series of questions. The questions suggested by the rites of various churches, although different in form, amount to the same
thing. They ask, in effect, "Are you willing to embrace all that
marriage demands?"

If you want to compose your own service, read the following examples as suggestions.

In the Episcopal service the questioning occurs at the very beginning of the service. After the procession and the greeting, the presider turns to the couple and asks the bride, "_____, will you have this man to be your husband; to live together in the covenant of marriage? Will you love him, comfort him, honor and keep him, in sickness and in health; and, forsaking all others, be faithful to him as long as you both shall live?" The presider then asks the groom the very same question (with the appropriate changes in pronouns, of course).

The Methodist service proposes the same question in different words: "_____, wilt thou have this woman to be thy wedded wife, to live together in the holy estate of matrimony? Wilt thou love her, comfort her, honor and keep her, in sickness and in health; and forsaking all others keep thee only unto her so long as ye both shall live?"

In the Presbyterian ritual the presider asks, "_____, wilt thou have this woman/man to be thy wife/husband, and wilt thou pledge thy troth to her/him, in all love and honor, in all duty and service, in all faith and tenderness, to live with her/him and cherish her/him, according to the ordinance of God, in the holy bond of marriage?"

The Roman Catholic service proposes three questions.

"_____ and _____, have you come here freely and without reservation to give yourselves to each other in marriage?" ("We have.")

"_____ and _____, will you love and honor each other as man and wife for the rest of your lives?" ("We will.")

"Will you accept children lovingly from God, and bring them up according to the law of Christ and his Church?" ("We will.")

The Community's Declaration of Consent

The Episcopal service introduces a brief question that slides by with little notice but that carries a lot of weight. After asking the couple to state their intention, the presider turns to the gathered community and asks them, "Will all of you witnessing these promises do all in your power to uphold these two persons in their marriage?" The question acknowledges a profound truth: Your relationship, as personal and intimate as it is, requires other people's support. Consider incorporating such a question into your service.

AFTER THE HOMILY I step out of the pulpit and directly address the congregation. I remind them that marriage is a communal undertaking. That their love and example has guided this couple to this moment. That this couple still needs their support. Then I ask them to stand up. And I ask them, "Do you pledge to uphold this couple with your continued love, assistance, wisdom, comfort, and encouragement?" There is usually a heartfelt though varied response—"I do," "We do," and "Yes." Then I say to the couple, "Surrounded by those you love and assured of their support, I ask you to step forward and state your intentions."

The Vows

In addition to the traditional form of the wedding vow, many churches and religious traditions have developed their own version. For example, the Episcopal church frames the well-known version with an introduction, "In the name of God, I, _____, take you, _____," and with a conclusion, "This is my solemn vow."

The Roman Catholic church allows couples to choose either the traditional form or a more contemporary version: "I, _____, take you, _____, to be my wife/husband. I promise to be true to you in good times and in bad, in sickness and in health. I will love you and honor you all the days of my life."

In an effort to personalize their ceremonies, some couples compose their own wedding vows.

Here are a few examples of personally composed vows.

"All that I am and all that I have, I offer to you, _____, in love and in joy. I, _____, take you, _____, to be my wife/husband, from this day forward. I will love and comfort you, hold you close, prize you above all others, and remain faithful to you all the days of our lives."

"I, _____, take you, _____, to be my partner in marriage and in life. I will love and honor you, stand by you and take your side, walk with you through life wherever it may lead, whatever may come. I will be father/mother to our children. I promise to be faithful and true from this day forward."

"I, _____, take you, _____, to myself, to have and to hold, to cherish and to honor, to support and to nurture, as husband/wife, lover, companion, friend, and, God willing, father/mother of my children. I promise you my never-ending love and faithfulness."

"With God as my witness, I, _____, take you, _____, as my husband/wife. I give myself to you, holding nothing back, promising you my love, devotion, and fidelity. I will love and cherish you every day of my life."

There's a lot to be said for relying on the traditional form of the wedding vow. It is traditional and, to a degree, universal. Married couples attending the ceremony will hear you speak the same words they spoke to each other and will feel more closely united to you as a result. They will also vicariously relive their own weddings and implicitly renew their own vows. The traditional vow is brief and to the point, and has a solid ring to it, while most personally composed vows tend to be long-winded and overly theoretical, theological, or psychological. They often sound tinny.

If you want to add a personal touch but you don't want to write your own vows, you could lead into them with your own words of introduction. It is hard to do so, however, without sounding trite and without adding clutter to something that is noble in its simplicity.

With This Ring

It is customary immediately after exchanging vows to exchange rings. Although in the past it was the man—and only the man—who gave his new wife a ring, today it is far more common and appropriate for each of you to give the other a ring.

There are two elements to this part of the ceremony: the blessing of the rings by the presider and the actual exchange of rings.

Blessing the Rings

We often think of a blessing as any good thing that we enjoy or that happens to us—our health, particular talents or personality traits, people we love, unexpected good fortune. But in the Bible blessings have a different meaning; they are whatever brings us closer to God. Since it's hard to measure God's nearness, the surest way to know if we've been blessed is to look for changes in our lives, changes that hint at new life.

God is the one who blesses. When we ourselves offer any sort of blessing—when we bless our food before eating it, for example—we are, in effect, giving thanks for gifts God has already given us.

If you plan on following the pattern of a traditional wedding, the presider will turn to one of your witnesses at the appropriate time and ask for the rings. With rings in hand, the presider will pray a brief blessing over them, asking God to bless them so that they may be both a symbol of married love and a means of deepening it. In some churches the presider may sprinkle them with holy water. If your ceremony is less formal or less religious in nature, you may simply omit the blessing and exchange the rings immediately after your vows without any interruption in the flow.

An English blessing dating back to the late Middle Ages sounds like this:

> Bless these rings, gracious Lord, that those who wear them, those who give and receive them, may be faithful to one another, remain in your peace, and live and grow old together in your love. Amen.

[The blessing of the rings in the Presbyterian and the Methodist church are slight variations on it.]

The contemporary blessing from the Episcopal Book of Common Prayer states:

> Bless, O Lord, these rings to be a sign of the vows by which this man and this woman have bound themselves to each other; through Jesus Christ our Lord. Amen.

The contemporary Roman Catholic ceremony suggests three different blessings:

> *May the Lord bless these rings*
> *which you give to each other*
> *as the sign of your love and fidelity.*

> *Lord, bless these rings which we bless in your name.*
> *Grant that those who wear them*
> *may always have a deep faith in each other.*
> *May they do your will*
> *and always live together*
> *in peace, good will, and love.*
> *We ask this through Christ our Lord.*

> *Lord,*
> *bless and consecrate _____ and _____*
> *in their love for each other.*
> *May these rings be a symbol*
> *of true faith in each other*
> *and always remind them of their love.*
> *Through Christ our Lord. Amen.*

If you have the opportunity to compose your own blessing, you might want to use one of these as a model:

> *Holy God, send your blessing upon these rings*
> *and upon _____ and _____, who wear them.*
> *Seal them with your love and make them unfailing in their*
>   *fidelity. Amen.*

> *Gracious God, source of countless blessings,*
> *look with favor on this couple*
> *and bless these rings.*
> *May they serve as a reminder of the holy vows they*
>   *exchanged today*
> *and seal them in your love.*

> *Holy God, bless these rings.*
> *As _____ and _____ wear them,*
> *may they remember their faith in you*
> *and their promises to each other.*
> *Let these rings be symbols of their deep and abiding love.*

After the rings have been blessed (or, if they aren't going to be blessed, immediately following your vows), you will place a ring on each other's finger, the ring finger of the left hand, and tell each other (briefly) what you mean by doing so.

As you think about what you want to say to each other while you're exchanging rings, remember that the rings themselves are a powerful symbol. The words are a reflection, and often a dim one at that, of the rings. You'll be better off avoiding the urge to "explain" their meaning or the meaning of what you are doing, since, as with most ritual moments, the exchange of rings almost speaks for itself. There is little need to embellish it with flowery sentiments or lengthy explanations.

The words you speak are meant for each other, words of the heart to accompany rings of precious metal.

Most church ceremonies suggest a simple declarative statement. The Lutheran service instructs the couple to say, "Receive this ring as a token of wedding love and troth." The Episcopal Book of Common Prayer, "I give you this ring as a symbol of my vow, and with all that I am, and all that I have, I honor you, in the name of the Father, and of the Son, and of the Holy Spirit." The Roman Catholic ritual, "Take this ring as a sign of my love and fidelity in the name of the Father, and of the Son, and of the Holy Spirit." The Baptist wording states, "With this ring I pledge my life and love to you in the name of the Father, and of the Son, and of the Holy Spirit." A Jewish ceremony states, "Behold thou art consecrated to me with this ring, according to the Law of Moses and Israel."

You could also say something like "See in this ring an outward sign of my heart's love and devotion" or "I give you this ring as I give you my love—to have and to hold from this day forward" or "May this ring be a sign and seal of the love that binds us together this day and forever." You could compose a variation on an older sentiment: "With this ring, I thee wed. I accept thee as my wife/husband. I endow thee with all my worldly goods. I acknowledge thee as my partner through the rest of my life. Thou art my beloved."

A practical note. Slipping a ring on another person's finger is not as easy as it sounds, especially when you are already nervous and have people staring intently at you. Your hands may well be shaking, and your ring fingers may be temporarily swollen. If this is the case, don't be upset. Simply place the ring on the finger as far as it will comfortably fit (past the first knuckle, hopefully). Then let the other person slip it on the rest of the way. (For some reason putting a ring on your own finger is always easier than putting it on another's.)

Prayers, Blessings, and Dismissal

By exchanging vows and rings, you marry yourselves in the presence of the community and the community's representative (the presider). It is then the community's turn to respond with words of prayer and blessing. Think of this concluding part of the rite as an outpouring of their love and good wishes for you.

Prayer

The presider will invite everyone present to pray on your behalf. Then, depending on the church's custom, the presider will voice petitions and ask for people's response ("amen" or "Lord, hear our prayer") or certain people you select will speak the petitions.

If at all possible, it is best to engage as many people as possible in voicing these prayers. Here are some alternatives:

- *The most common form followed by many churches is also the simplest. A person steps forward to the place where earlier the readings were proclaimed. He or she reads three or four petitions that have already been composed, asking after each one for the people's assent. A slight variation has two people coming forward at the same time, perhaps a favorite couple, and taking turns reading the petitions.*

- *After the person (or couple) has read several petitions, they might add an invitation to the entire assembly. "If you wish to speak aloud some prayer, please do so now." To encourage people to speak up, you might want to prime the pump. Tell a few of your more extroverted friends and relatives beforehand what you mean to do so that they can think of a prayer to voice "spontaneously" when the time comes. This form works best in small to medium-sized weddings, especially where people are grouped close together.*

- *You could arrange for four or five people to speak a petition from their places in the congregation. Doing so makes it clear that the prayers are coming from the people themselves. Again, you could have the person who reads the last petition invite prayers from the rest of the community.*

Throughout the centuries Christians (and mystics from other religious traditions) have recognized "petitionary prayer" as one of the mainstays of authentic prayer. (The others are praise, thanksgiving, and adoration.) Jesus taught his followers to pray with complete assurance that their prayers will be answered; God treats us with a love even greater than that of parents for their children. Since we believe that God cares for us and desires our welfare, we have every right to make known our cares, concerns, aspirations. Asking another for a favor, after all, is an expression of trust and vulnerability, so go ahead and make your requests known.

A prayer of petition is simple to compose. In its simplest form it is a wish or a hope addressed to God.

Here are some examples to serve as models for your own. Be sure to adapt them so that they reflect your particular concerns and needs.

- *Gracious God, we ask your blessings upon _____ and _____, who begin their lives as husband and wife today. Give them joy in each other's presence, perseverance in hardship, consolation in grief, good health, and long life in the company of many friends.* Amen.
- *We pray, too, for all who have brought them to this moment in their lives by their loving examples (here you might want to mention several important people, your parents, perhaps, by name). For their faithfulness and love, bless them with your grace and peace.* Amen.
- *We pray for those who could not be physically present today but who are with us in love and prayers, especially (mention by name your favorite relatives and friends who couldn't be with you because of distance, expense, or illness). May their love be returned many times over.* Amen.
- *We pray in loving memory for those we love who have died and*

who surround us still with their care (list close relatives and friends by name). Amen.

- Please add your own prayers aloud, if you wish, or in the silence of your hearts.

The Episcopal Book of Common Prayer gives these prayers:

- Eternal God, creator and preserver of all life, author of salvation, and giver of all grace: Look with favor upon the world you have made, and for which your Son gave his life, and especially upon this man and this woman whom you make one flesh in Holy Matrimony. Amen.

- Give them wisdom and devotion in the ordering of their common life, that each may be to the other a strength in need, a counselor in perplexity, a comfort in sorrow, and a companion in joy. Amen.

- Grant that their wills may be so knit together in your will, and their spirits in your Spirit, that they may grow in love and peace with you and one another all the days of their life. Amen.

- Give them grace, when they hurt each other, to recognize and acknowledge their fault, and to seek each other's forgiveness and yours. Amen.

- Make their life together a sign of Christ's love to this sinful and broken world, that unity may overcome estrangement, forgiveness heal guilt, and joy conquer despair. Amen.

- Bestow on them, if it is your will, the gift and heritage of children, and the grace to bring them up to know you, to love you, and to serve you. Amen.

- Give them such fulfillment of their mutual affection that they may reach out in love and concern for others. Amen.

- *Grant that all married persons who have witnessed these vows may find their lives strengthened and their loyalties confirmed.* Amen.

- *Grant that the bonds of our common humanity by which all your children are united one to another, and the living to the dead, may be so transformed by your grace that your will may be done on earth as it is in heaven; where, O Father, with your Son and the Holy Spirit, you live and reign in perfect unity, now and for ever.* Amen.

The Lord's Prayer

The best way to conclude the prayers of petition is to invite everyone present to join in the Lord's Prayer (also called the "Our Father" by Catholics). It is the only prayer attributed to Jesus himself and, as brief as it is, the one prayer that best sums up our dependence on God. Throughout the centuries commentators have attributed nearly mystical power to the prayer—the ability to unite all who recite it together, to forgive sins, and to insure lasting peace. On a practical level it is the one prayer that almost every person at your wedding will be able to say.

Your presider might simply conclude the petitions with this segue, "We unite all our prayers with the prayer Jesus gave us as we say together, 'Our Father . . .' "

The Blessing

The nuptial blessing concludes and crowns the wedding rite. In many church services (Presbyterian, Baptist, and Methodist, for example) the presider blesses everyone, the couple and the community together, using the most ancient prayer of blessing recorded in the Bible:

The Lord bless and keep you.
The Lord make his face to shine upon you,
and be gracious to you.
The Lord lift up his countenance upon you,
and give you peace. Amen.

NUMBERS 6:24–26

In other services the presider prays a blessing directly over the couple and then blesses the entire community before sending everyone forth.

The presider could invite everyone present to join in praying the blessing over you by asking them to extend their right hands out in your direction (the ancient sign of blessing).

The Lutheran Prayer Over the Couple

Almighty, everlasting God, our heavenly Father,
having joined this man and woman in holy marriage,
grant that by your blessing they may live together
according to your word and promise.
Strengthen them in faithfulness and love toward each other.
Sustain and defend them in all trial and temptation,
and help them to live in faith toward you
in the communion of your holy church
and in loving service to each other
that they may ever enjoy your blessing,
through Jesus Christ, your son, our Lord,

who lives and reigns with you and the Holy Spirit,
one God, now and forever. Amen.

The Episcopal Prayer Over the Couple

Most gracious God,
we give you thanks for your tender love
in sending Jesus Christ to come among us,
to be born of a human mother,
and to make the way of the cross to be the way of life.
We thank you, also,
for consecrating the union of man and woman in his name.
By the power of your Holy Spirit,
pour out the abundance of your blessing
upon this man and this woman.
Defend them from every enemy.
Lead them into all peace.
Let their love for each other be a seal upon their hearts,
a mantle about their shoulders,
and a crown upon their foreheads.
Bless them in their work and in their companionship;
in their sleeping and in their waking;
in their joys and in their sorrows;
in their life and in their death.
Finally, in your mercy,
bring them to that table where your saints feast for ever
in your heavenly home;
through Jesus Christ, our Lord,
who with You and the Holy Spirit lives and reigns,
one God, for ever and ever. Amen.

THE NUPTIAL BLESSING:

God the Father, God the Son, God the Holy Spirit,
bless, preserve, and keep you;
the Lord mercifully with his favor look upon you,
and fill you with all spiritual benediction and grace;
that you may faithfully live together in this life,
and in the age to come have life everlasting. Amen.

The Roman Catholic Nuptial Blessing

May almighty God, with his word of blessing,
unite your hearts in the never-ending bond of pure love.
  Amen.

May your children bring you happiness,
and may your generous love for them
be returned to you, many times over. Amen.

May the peace of Christ live always in your hearts and in
  your home.
May you have true friends to stand by you, both in joy and
  in sorrow.
May you be ready and willing to help and comfort
all who come to you in need.
And may the blessings promised to the compassionate
be yours in abundance. Amen.

May you find happiness and satisfaction in your work.
May daily problems never cause you undue anxiety,
nor the desire for earthly possessions dominate your lives.

*But may your hearts' first desire be always the good things
waiting for you in the life of heaven.* Amen.

*May the Lord bless you with many happy years together,
so that you may enjoy the rewards of a good life.
And after you have served him loyally in his kingdom on
     earth,
may he welcome you to his eternal kingdom in heaven.*
     Amen.

Dismissal

The entire service concludes with the dismissal by the presider,
who says, in effect, "You're married! Go now and be a light to
the world." And that's what you do. You take each other by the
arm and walk out to the most joyful, the grandest fanfare the organ or musicians can provide—and, typically, to the spontaneous
applause of your guests. Then everyone—your witnesses, your
families, and all the rest—follow after you.

The Celebration Continues—
the Reception

With the recessional, the sacred celebration comes to an end and everyone steps over the threshold from the sacred ceremonies to the social celebrations of the reception. If you are leaving a church that has bells, now is the time to have them rung out over the community. Church bells contribute a sense of exhilarating declaration.

Now everything breaks wide open with music, dancing, eating, and toasts. In fact, the wedding reception has many of the symbolic gestures and components that the solemn ceremony does. *People:* There is your entry as a new husband and wife central to the feast. It has the guests wishing you well, participating in the action and rejoicing with you. *Symbol:* There is wine taken in ceremony and a cake—no ordinary cake—shared with ceremony. Your hospitality continues through the feast. There are gifts brought to you with love and good wishes. *Space:* There is the garden, the hall, the house, the room that becomes re-created into a festive place for the reception. There are flowers or streamers, balloons or banners to define the space. *Story:* There are formalized statements, stories, memories, and toasts offered. There might be a photo story on the walls that tells something of the early history of the bride and the groom. People may contribute ballads or poems. *Action:* There is music and dancing and visiting. And then there is your ritualized departure. So many aspects of a reception mirror what you just celebrated more solemnly only a short time earlier. This time, however, the festive spirit is more relaxed and playful.

The reception, just as the sacred celebration, needs careful planning but also a little abandon to allow something fresh to happen if it will. In your plans, you will probably look at the cus-

---

SO IT REALLY WASN'T our style—the garter, the bouquet, the going-away car, all that. But I saw how important it was to my new mother-in-law-to-be and I thought: What the heck. Let's just do it. It's no skin off our teeth, if it makes her happy—we can do that much.

WE TOSSED OUT everything that wasn't relevant to our personal values. No garters, no bouquet tossing, no money dance, etc. We don't try and get all our single friends married. We don't need charity (give to those who do).

toms, traditions, or rituals that have attached themselves to wedding receptions. Some are old. Some are newer. Some have lost their meaning, taken superstitious overtones, or smack of practices that are sexist, have lost their propriety, or fail to be in good taste. This is the place where you can introduce what is more personally your own, or ethnically yours. But everything you consider you will want to carefully examine. Does it stand on its own? Is it a clear statement of who you are? Is it in good taste? Does it need to be reframed, is there something to be retrieved and reintroduced, or should this be thrown out?

People

ENTRY — You will want to arrive in the hall as soon as possible after the guests have arrived. As both hosts and guests of honor, you set the tone and allow the festivities to begin in earnest. Little is more anticlimactic or disappointing than to wait around too long for photographers to pose their shots after the service, holding up the guests and possibly delaying the feast. As the bride and groom, you will probably feel eager to get back to your guests and be part of the party. (See the section on photography.) An uncertain or blurry beginning takes energy from the tone and spirit of a celebration. The more you can do to clarify or define the end of one phase of your celebration and the beginning of the reception, the more comfortable everyone feels.

When it's possible, it helps to have the solemn ceremony and the reception geographically close to each other or even on the same grounds—as in the church courtyard or the parish hall. Sometimes it seems to break the spell to interrupt the celebrations with a commute across town. On the other hand, sometimes such an intermission is an opportunity to contemplate what has just occurred before you lurch into the next round of celebrations.

SOME OF OUR FRIENDS, aware that their relatives and friends had come from far and near and that this opportunity to visit with such an array of friends is rare, reserved a group of cottages at a lake country resort. After the wedding ceremony, we regrouped at the resort lodge for feasting and dancing. Then we all stayed the night at the various cottages and next morning had a great buffet brunch, and a chance to play golf, tennis, go boating, or go on a hike. A lot of their aunts and uncles hung around the big old front porch of the lodge and enjoyed the sunshine and the porch rockers. We all enjoyed each other until early afternoon. Then it was time to check out.

THEY MARRIED on the East Coast, where the wife is from. And all the groom's friends and family are on the West Coast. So after the wedding they returned west and had a reception for all the people who couldn't go east. They put together a slide show of carefully edited pictures that showed the whole thing—their wedding in a small town in Vermont and all the preparations that went before it. Their parents all stayed at the bride's parents' lake cabin. All the young folk stayed in two little cabins across the lake. It seemed perfect—they went back and forth by rowboat. The bride wore her mother's wedding dress and the groom's four sisters helped her adjust and refit it. So they had pictures of that project. The moms picked flowers in the woods and made a wreath for the bride and bouquets for all the groom's sisters. There were wonderful pictures of the moms in the woods in their rain jackets in pouring rain picking wildflowers. There were pictures of all the guys goofing off and clowning at the end of the dock. There were kitchen pictures of the cake being baked in an old stove. The little kids had rustled up a ball game and they had pictures of them all muddy and grand.

The morning of the wedding, before anyone was up, the groom took his mom out real early for a boat ride on the lake when the water was glassy and a mist hung over it. She told about that several times over the next months because it really touched her—a really good talk with her son before the wedding mayhem began. Then the mists burned off and it was time to dress—and there are pictures of young folk running about in slips and lining up for the iron. But the very best were fabulous pictures of the wedding party traveling on foot over a grassy meadow along the edge of the wood to the church. They walked about a block into town to a little white church in the square, where the priest was waiting for them at the door and everybody just walked in, took seats, and then the bride and groom followed, surrounded by his sisters and brothers and all the parents. Three in that family are really good with cameras, so the slide show for their West Coast reception was brilliant and it was fun to see it and hear all the stories.

Action

MUSIC—Some couples hire an emcee (or a lovely extroverted uncle takes the role!) to keep the festivities flowing. Other couples consider an emcee an intrusion—a "hired voice" who may take over or manipulate the tone and spirit of things in a way they do not feel represents them. When you don't have a live band, you might ask a disc jockey to keep things moving but without too much other interjection of personality. Maybe you have friends who play music or sing and would want to make a contribution of music toward the entertainment.

This is the place more appropriate for those show tunes or popular music that would have been out of place in the sacred ceremonies. Perhaps there is a grandpa who plays accordion, or an uncle who plays the bagpipes. Or perhaps you are the kind who would like to hire a square dance caller or someone to teach some folk dances to get everyone on their feet and interacting. Many young people know how to select dance music that is good for the whole range of ages represented. Some couples hire a chamber group to play classical music while people mingle and meet one another, and break out the wild music when everyone is ready to dance. This is an area where your individual tastes have a wide range for expression.

FIRST DANCE—One of the practices we see frequently is the first dance of the newly married couple. It has thrown any number of engaged couples into panic, making them take lessons in ballroom dancing so they can perform a dance for all to see without falling all over themselves. Ballroom dancing has not often been part of the experience of modern young people. Who knows, but that this waltz may be the first and last time they will ever dance it. Being on display and the object of everyone's attention might be very uncomfortable for some couples, or for one of the two of you. Here you can be creative. The first dance of the new wife and husband carries the symbolism of their ability to be in harmony with each other, but if one of you simply has two left feet, it should cast no aspersions on the rest of your communication style. Dance any way you are comfortable.

If you have asked someone to teach the group folk dances, line dances, Greek dances, or circle dances, you might invent a less awkward alternative to the first dance. Improvise a snake dance with the two of you going about picking up one guest after the other to follow behind with linked arms. Lead everyone about the place. Or have everyone invited to dance around you in a circle to something lively and loosening.

Well-chosen and well-presented dance music gives everyone

THE EMCEE WAS A PLEASANT FELLOW, though I have no idea who he was or where he came from. He got the bride and groom set up very graciously for their "first dance," routines and as more and more people joined in the dancing, he made this announcement. He said that wedding reception practices had been concerned too long with getting the single people married off—"with our bouquet and garter rites"—and we didn't celebrate married people enough. So he asked everyone present who was married to get up and come to the dance floor. As they danced to the music, he called off numbers very slowly. "One!" and all the people who were married for one year were asked to leave the dance floor. "Two!" and on through the years until fewer and fewer couples remained on the floor. There was this increased intensity as the numbers climbed. Everyone was watching the couples who were still out there. The couples gazed in each other's eyes with more feeling and silent understanding. Finally we were at numbers 57 and 58. And there were two dear little couples left: the groom's grandparents and his great-great-aunt and uncle. The music had slowed way down and then ended with a clash of cymbals and the people cheered and whistled and clapped. It was so lovely and very touching!

the most natural way to break out of any stiffness left over from the ceremony and just cut loose. Ties come off. Jackets are tossed across the backs of chairs, cummerbunds are cast aside, and women finally take off their shoes. With all the care, solemnity, and awareness that has preceded this part of the celebration, something of the opposite, the wild and lively and the unexpected, finds place for expression. And so it must.

Story

T O A S T S—At one time, making a toast was a common, even daily custom. Now the practice has become less frequent or reserved for formal occasions. Inexperience, unfamiliarity, or nervousness causes some people who propose toasts at a wedding to hurry through them or undercut their significance. With planning and thoughtfulness, however, toasts add a courtesy and a touch of affection to receptions as well as to the rehearsal dinner that goes before. And, of course, men aren't the only ones who propose toasts.

Etiquette calls for the best man to propose a toast to the bride and the groom at the beginning of the reception and for the groom to follow the best man with a toast of his own to his bride. Since etiquette must shift to reflect contemporary sensibilities and social realities, there is no limit on who can offer a toast to whom. Why should the bride or any other woman be kept silent? Unless, of course, she is shy and would rather be spared the embarrassment of being the focus of attention.

In ancient times the Greeks and Romans, before taking a drink, poured a small amount of wine onto the ground or on the table as an offering to the gods. They did so either in silent homage or with a brief prayer in praise of the god they wished to honor.

THE GROOM PROPOSED a moving toast to the gathered friends, thanking them for coming—some from very far away—for their love and support, and asking them to remain close, because every marriage, he said, was as good as the community of people that supported and blessed it. We need one another, he said, to make this world the best place it can be for us and for those who come after us.

Blessed art Thou, O Lord our God, King of the universe, who hath created the fruit of the vine.

Blessed art Thou, O Lord our God, King of the universe, who creates many living beings and the things they need.

For all that Thou hast created to sustain the life of every living being, blessed be Thou, the Life of the universe.

For the Jewish people in Old Testament times, meals were a sacred event. Food shared with others, they believed, fed the whole person, body and soul. At meals festive enough to include wine, the host raised the first cup and praised God, the source of all blessings. The host sipped from it, passed it around the table, and invited everyone present to drink from it. Those who drank from the common cup were bound as if by a sacred oath to live together in peace. At the last supper Jesus followed this same custom when he took a cup filled with wine, raised it in blessing, and gave it to his disciples.

The custom of raising and touching glasses with the others just after a toast is ancient. Due to the varied effects alcohol had on those who drank it, ancient people believed that evil spirits entered the body along with the drink. They clinked their glasses together to make a noise, believing that noise frightened demons away. When we honk horns, blow whistles, or shoot off firecrackers on New Year's Eve, we practice a remnant of that old superstition. The tin cans tied to the car of the bride and groom, and the honking of horns has its roots in the same superstition: Make a din and keep away the evil spirits.

And speaking of keeping evil spirits at bay, it is, in fact, wise for you, the bride and groom, to remember to eat something in the midst of all these festivities. You may have been too excited to eat and the spirits in toasts will be difficult to handle on an empty stomach.

Toasts at a wedding reception bind together the people present in an expression of affection and goodwill for the bride and groom. Clinking glasses may or may not chase away evil spirits from the start of their new life, but it does surround the married couple with cheerful assurances of love and support.

Brief toasts are often the best. And if you are unaccustomed to public declarations, all the better to keep the toast short. A few carefully chosen words clearly and lovingly stated is a blessing for all. A little sentimentality, better avoided on other occasions, is perfectly acceptable at both the rehearsal dinner and the reception. Humor can add sparkle and laughter to toasts, but it should never embarrass the couple or the guests. (Double entendres and sexual references, the hallmark of bachelor parties, are inappropriate at a wedding reception.) It is always wiser to poke fun at yourself than to make others the object of laughter.

Toasts tend to have a prescribed, though flexible, format. They resemble short speeches with an introduction, a body, and a conclusion.

How to Propose a Toast

First, get everyone's attention. Introduce yourself briefly. "I've known Jacob for the past seven years, ever since we were roommates in college." "As the father of the bride . . ." "I'm Elizabeth's elder sister."

Next, propose the toast. State one wish or hope for the couple. The subjunctive mood ("may") works well. "May Maggie and Jim find happiness, prosperity, and love in all the years to come." A simple declarative sentence also works. "To Helen and Ed—a lovely bride, a handsome groom—and the happiest couple I know."

Finally, conclude the toast by raising your glass, saying, "To the bride and groom" or "To Vanessa and Lloyd."

From introduction to conclusion, toasts need take no more than thirty seconds. If you write it out (so that you can memorize it beforehand), it need count no more than fifty to seventy-five words.

On the other hand, if you are a skilled public speaker with exquisite taste in literature and the mood is right, you may choose to read a carefully selected segment of poetry. If you are a recognized poet, you might even write a poem for the occasion if you don't succumb to using the occasion as your personal platform. Nothing is more embarrassing than the long-winded airbag who loves the sound of his own voice and goes on and on. Brevity is the soul of wit. It's also the soul of a very good toast.

CLEARLY, the best man was beside himself with the anticipation of proposing the toast. I saw him pacing along the side of the building, loosening his tie and mumbling to himself. He was memorizing his words. Taking the whole thing terribly seriously. And then he stood there, got our attention, stuttered a bit with bashfulness, and then lost himself in a passage from Pablo Neruda. Lost himself! It was stunning. Could have heard a pin drop. Some couple I didn't know, standing just behind me, whispered one to the other: "Let's get married all over again and get this guy to be our best man."

Here are some examples of short toasts. (Remember to add your own introduction and conclusion.)

"To Doreen and Bill—may the happiness of this day and the love they share grow stronger, brighter, and riper with every day."

"To the bride and groom—may they find in their love for each other happiness enough to share with all."

"May Martha and Andrew be blessed with loving children, faithful friends, work they enjoy, and many years of happiness in each other's love."

"To Susan and Martin—my favorite oldest daughter and my favorite newest son."

"To the woman whose love makes me happier than I ever thought or imagined I could be."

"To Peter, my wonderful husband, who has captured my heart and fills me to the brim with joy."

The whole toast, from beginning to end, might sound like this: "Justin has been my great friend since sixth grade. I never knew a more faithful friend. Please raise your glasses to Justin and his beautiful bride, Beckie. May their home be filled with laughter that cheers the heart and a love that makes all burdens light. To Beckie and Justin."

SOME CLEVER PERSON had two slide projectors going against the wall in the dining hall. Side by side they automatically flashed pictures against the wall: the grandparents on their wedding days, the parents getting married, the bride and groom as babies, toddlers, grammar-school kids, scouts, 4-H, with their pets. Halloween—everything side by side! Prom pictures, class plays, graduation. It was a riot! Someone spent a lot of time matching the two through every stage of their growing up. It grabbed a lot of attention and elicited some great stories—especially as some of the friends they had when they were kids were both in the pictures and also at the wedding. That would be a very nice wedding gift to a couple—to arrange some kind of photo display like that—something a sibling from each side of the family could contribute. I've seen it done with two posters side by side for the two of them. And I've seen framed pictures sitting on a table of a great-grand-mother, grandmother, mother—on their wedding days wearing the gown that now the daughter wears on her wedding day. That was fascinating to look at.

THERE WERE BASKETS stacked with disposable cameras. Everywhere you were during the reception, you could just reach for a camera and take a shot of something you thought you'd like to record for the married couple. Then you dropped the camera off again. It made for a lot of great and funny pictures for the couple's scrap books! You got a really good sense of what was going on around the reception. It's certainly a lot easier to edit out a pile of snapshots like that than long videos that never seem to get edited.

Stories

Stories abound at weddings, in part, because old friends reconnect and begin reminiscing. People will often supply a wall of photos from the lives of the bride and groom, which inspires conversations and story sharing.

Glass Clanking Reframed

A rather recent "custom," which may be a variation of the clinking of glasses after a toast, consists in all the guests clanking on their glasses with a fork. It insists the bride and groom kiss.

FRANKLY, IT'S NOT A CUTE PRACTICE. We felt really stupid and controlled. Because you don't always have a say about these things—someone is very likely to get it going—and then what can you do? We just make a game of it and were sports. But we would have preferred it be more civilized. Actually, we've been to a couple of weddings recently where no one did it! Maybe it's on the wane? Or maybe other couples like it and we're just the odd ones out?

WHEN MY STEPDAUGHTER married, she was concerned that the folks she invited didn't know one another very well and that conversation at the tables might be awkward, so she wanted something to break the ice. Instead of that insane glass-clanking routine, where the bride and groom have to kiss on command, each table was asked to serenade the bride and groom with a love song—or a poem. Then the bride and groom kissed. We made these little "do-it-yourself toast kits." Each table was presented with a champagne flute containing a lovely piece of embossed stationery and a gold pencil tied up in netting and silk ribbons and silk rosebuds. Then her zany dad, acting as emcee, invited everyone at their tables to put their heads together, share information about the couple, and come up with a toast or a song or a poem for the bride and groom. Throughout the dinner, when a table indicated they were ready by clanking their glasses, he invited folks to come up and present their creation. One group sang a song making a pun out of their new last hyphenated names with all their own made-up lyrics which were wonderful. Another table recited a "roses are red" poem, etc. It was great fun and sheer delight for the newlyweds. You need a good emcee to get and keep things going and to stir up the creativity. And at the end of it all, the bride and groom get a wonderful set of champagne flutes for their first New Year's party together. And all the little songs and lyrics were written down on the papers for them to keep.

Space

The reception area is a space that you somehow re-create for the occasion. Some spaces need more ideas and work than others to transform them. If you are in a grand open space, you can define an area within it to better contain your party. Getting too spread out and diluted separates the guests from one another, hinders conversation, and destroys the sense of a "critical mass" of celebrating participants.

A ceremony held on the vast lawns of a college campus was greatly enhanced and brightly defined by having been bounded with tall bamboo poles planted in a circle. At the top of the poles a fluttering bunch of crepe paper streamers flowed out into the wind and added festive color and movement. At the bottom of each pole there was a gathered bunch of wild mustard tied in place that had the look of yellow lace. The effect was to make a "room" in the open space. They had incorporated two large trees into the edge of the circle and had strung up a brightly woven cloth between the trees to form a focal backdrop for the head table.

THE TABLES WERE SET out in a U shape. Everyone could see everyone else. In the middle of the U a temporary dance floor had been set up and a band had created their own stage at the far end of the circle. It meant that you could watch the dancing if you weren't dancing yourself—something I noticed that the older people appreciated. They liked being near the action but not necessarily in the thick of it.

THE BRIDE AND HER MOM planted many little baskets with various herbs and tucked moss all around them. They kept them moist and growing until the day of the wedding. Then they tucked fresh blossoms among the herbs and ribbons coming out of the pots with the meaning of each of the herbs lettered on them. Those were the centerpieces for the tables and the gifts the bride gave to all the people who had helped her with the wedding or who were special to her in bringing her to this moment.

THE NEIGHBORS had a beautiful tree with heart-shaped burgundy leaves. I think it was called Red Bud. At their suggestion, we put one leaf on the plate or napkin of each guest and sprigs of the same into the centerpieces.

HERE'S WHAT WE DID: At the center of each table at the reception there was a wide clay pot tied with raffia. It contained a bundle of fresh fir seedlings—one for each guest to take home and plant and tend in honor of their own relationships and for the good of the earth.

WE USED little four-by-four-inch florist pots of pink and red and orange impatiens. We hid them inside lined baskets and added fresh baby's breath at the last minute. It was pretty, inexpensive, and we could plant them in our gardens when the festivities were over.

Where the climate so dictates, you will likely plan for an indoor reception—or at least the possibility of open shelter if you have a summer shower. Being inside causes us to bring something of the outdoors in. Flowers, plants, trees, table centerpieces, etc. Inside, too, there are situations that need a little definition and containment. You will also want to have a focal point—for the cake and the toasts. If you are in a hall with a stage or platform, use it to elevate the focus so everyone can see you.

The arrangement of tables and guests is usually dictated by circumstances and preference. Some couples don't like to be the focus at a head table but would prefer to be among the other guests at any table. Some use place cards to arrange and mix guests, others let people arrange themselves. In any case, you will want, as gracious hosts, to mingle among your guests, taking a moment to chat with them all between courses or dances. This seems to be the direction the earlier "receiving lines" have taken. It is a less formal solution to meeting and greeting everyone. It also puts some of the responsibility on the guests to approach you, introduce themselves if they are long-lost relatives, and greet you.

As there always are a goodly number of older people among your guests, it is thoughtful to have a place where they can also escape the loud music but still be a part of things. Or consider lowering the volume to a thoughtful decibel for ears that are not used to loud music.

Gifts

Some couples have lived independently for a time and have a considerable amount of household appointments already between them. It's not like starting out as eighteen-year-olds without a stick to their names. Or they may not wish on principle to own many things. If the two of you are among those who may wish to travel light and live responsibly on this earth, indicate this to your friends. Suggest a favorite charity or cause to which you'd like them to contribute in your name.

Symbol

A MEAL PRAYER—Before the meal is served, some couples ask the person who married them or another person to offer a prayer. Here's a great moment to involve someone like a godmother, a mentor, or favorite teacher. A blessing is perfectly appropriate here, more especially when there has been no Eucharistic feast celebrated in the church, or solemn part of your ceremony. The wedding feast has special power and energy in it whether it is

---

THEY DIDN'T WANT any gifts and they suggested a few ecologically sound projects that we could contribute to instead. They aren't rich—they don't have a lot of stuff. But they said they didn't *want* a lot of stuff. They want to live simply and not be loaded down with boxes of possessions—especially when they don't have a house yet to put it in. But their attitude was a far cry from all those letters to Dear Abby, where you read about out-of-control "greedy brides." Or ungrateful ones. We did give them a little something, but it was a very good feeling to send a check to the Nature Conservancy in their name. The wedding and reception had that same responsible, solid feel to it. Simple, hearty, and we had a wonderful time.

IN FACT, we tried to ask for no gifts, but no one would cooperate with that one. So then we asked the people to give their favorite book or CD. No one liked that either. We ended up with lots of platters.

---

catered, cooked by the parish women, or a pot luck of everyone's prize recipes. A wedding feast nourishes on many levels. To offer a meal prayer creates a small, gracious circle around this event of sharing and eating and rejoicing over food together. If the beginning of the meal is an awkward time to suggest a blessing—because it is a buffet meal, for instance—choose a different kind of blessing to offer at the time of the cutting of the cake. (See page 213.)

Here are some meal prayers you can consider:

Bless us, O Lord,
and these thy gifts
which we are about to receive,
from thy bounty.
Through Christ, our Lord. Amen

Lord, bless this food for our use
and us for your service.
May the food renew our strength,
give energy to our bodies,
new thought to our minds.
May this wine restore our souls,
give vision and joy to our spirits,
and warmth to the love in our hearts.
And once refreshed,
may we use our whole selves,
mind and body,
heart and spirit
to proclaim your great glory. Amen

Bless Bride and Groom,
And bless us too,
And bless this food
Which we enjoy.
Through Christ, our Lord.
Amen

O Thou, who clothes the lilies,
And feeds the birds of the sky,
Who leads the lambs to pasture,
And the deer to the waterside,
Who multiplies loaves and fishes,
And at a wedding changed water to wine,
Please join us at our table,
As giver and guest, to dine.

Give to the hungry some of your bread
and to the naked some of your clothing.
Seek counsel from every wise person.
At all times bless the Lord,
and ask God to make straight all your paths
and to grant success to all your
endeavors and plans.
For this we pray. Amen.

ADAPTED FROM TOBIT 4:16–19

Lord, put bread on the table of those who are hungry.
And for those who have bread, make them hungry for justice.

With a small preface, thanking the bride and groom for their hospitality, remind them, and all present, always to extend hospitality to others:

I saw a stranger today.
I put food for him in the eating place
And drink in the drinking place.
In the Holy Name of the Trinity
He blessed myself and my house
My goods and my family.
And the lark said in her warble
Often, often, often
Goes Christ in the stranger's guise.
O, oft and oft and oft,
Goes Christ in the stranger's guise.

CELTIC RUNE OF HOSPITALITY

May love, joy, and peace be _____'s and _____'s in
*   abundance*
and may it be so for us all. Amen.
May their home be made holy, O God, by your light.
May the light of love and truth shine upon them and us all.
May their table and this one be blessed by your holy presence
at this meal and every meal. Amen.

Eat your bread with joy and drink with a merry heart,
because it is now that God looks upon you with favor.
*   Amen.*

Peace between neighbors
Peace between kindred,
Peace between lovers,
In the love of the king of life.
Peace between person and person,
Peace between wife and husband,
Peace between women and children.
The peace of Christ above all peace.

CELTIC BLESSING

Blessings for the Cutting of the Cake

The sharing of food between the bride and the groom is one of the truly ancient and consistently universal symbols enacted at a wedding ceremony. It reflects the sharing of bread and wine in communion. It makes of the two, companions for life, *companion* meaning the one you share your bread with. By further sharing the cake with all the guests, it invites the entire group to become companions in the sharing of this food. It is intimacy and an invitation to community all in a single sign.

If it is easier to offer a short blessing at the time of the cake cutting, it would be a fine gesture to invite all the guests to participate by extending a hand in the direction of the couple as the leader says one of these blessings:

May the blessings of God rest upon you,
May God's peace abide with you,
May God's presence illuminate your hearts
Now and forevermore.

SUFI BLESSING

Loving God,
let this table
be a sign of tomorrow's hope already here,
Let this festive wedding cake
remind us of that great feast
where justice and peace will reign forever. Amen

IN THE PARISH hall with its high, dark rafters—there over the table where the wedding cake would stand—they hung a wreath down from the rafters to circle above the cake. The wreath was tucked with ferns and spring flowers. From the ceiling, through the center of the wreath or spilling over its sides, it rained down yards and yards of shimmering ribbons. And hanging from the wreath itself were five bright apples. It had something of the look of a maypole about it and it certainly brought attention to the cake and made a focal point in that vast room.

Cake Cutting

With the cutting of the cake, certain superstitions and sexist manifestations crop up—who has the "upper hand" and such. To make matters worse, this is one of those times when the photographer seems to become particularly busy posing you over and over again. You may want to speak to the photographer beforehand and ask that there be a limit to the number of times you have to retake that shot. For the sake of equality, you may want to invent new forms of cake cutting. Cutting a single piece from two sides with two knives and sharing it. Sharing it with linked arms. Cutting with interlocked arms and a single knife? Have fun with it and be inventive.

The obvious "tradition" you may want to look at again is this relatively recent invention of "cake smushing." While it is true that so much has been poised and proper, gracious and courteous, in good taste and considerate something will probably give. "Cake smushing"—usually perpetrated against one person by the other—does nothing to grace the occasion. The place to let go and loosen up is with the music and dancing. Not the food. Sharing a piece of this cake tenderly and lovingly is a significant and holy act. It is a kind of Eucharist which you then invite all your guests to share.

I THINK THE GUY was so sick of being led around by the women who planned everything—so sick of the frilly and the frou-frou that his hostility and immaturity just came out. He really went after that poor bride, and it was not a pretty thing. Possibly, if the groom had had more involvement and an equal part in planning and preparing, he would have taken some ownership in that wedding.

WE WERE FEEDING a morsel of cake to one another and a bunch of guys at the back of the room began to chant: Smush it in her face! Smush it in her face! We ignored them.

Bouquet and Garter

Two traditions that inspire discarding, unless you have a fabulous way of reframing them, is throwing the bouquet to the unmarried women and the garter to the bachelors. Throwing the bouquet to unmarried women with the idea that the one who catches it will be the next to marry is demeaning of women, of the single state, and of marriage. An alternative to consider would be handing your bouquet to someone there who has been very important in your life as a sign of gratitude and love. This could be your grandfather, your little brother, your boss, a former teacher, your mother. Many people have been part of your experience and have contributed in ways they didn't even notice to the development of the person you have become today. This might be a fine way to thank that person.

There was a time when the groom's masculinity was measured by how quickly he could deflower his bride after the wedding. Bits of her clothing were pitched over the balustrade to the cheering crowd below as some sign of his "progress." Since the garter practice has to do with a different time and a different attitude toward women, virginity, and marriage, it seems particularly out of place in a thoughtful and mutually respectful wedding.

NO WAY that garter routine! I can't believe it hasn't died a natural death. Why would I want to treat my wife like that in public? You've seen it where the guy pulls off the garter with his teeth? Actually I've noticed that among my colleagues it hasn't occurred. It might be an education thing. Graduate students are beyond that stuff?

Going Away

When it is time for you to end the festivities and bring the day to a close, your friends will gather around you to see you off and cheer you on your way. This is the moment to come to each of your parents and say good-bye and thank them. It is an outward sign of a new relationship you have with them of respect and gratitude and indicates your new allegiance to your spouse. Take your time with them. Ask them for their blessing. And then grab your spouse around the waist and dash off to your waiting car to wave and cheer and collapse someplace peaceful. You'll find yourselves reviewing and cross-checking your observations and impressions for some time to come. And so you should. This is no day to forget easily. The car you drove off in may or may not have been decorated by your friends. There seems little reason to rent some exotic antique car to make your getaway as some people do. Remember, those aren't the symbols that carry meaning. They only add stress to your budget and logistical complications to your day.

IT WAS SO IMPORTANT to my new mother-in-law that we have a picture of us taking off in the car and being waved to by all the guests. So we actually took off in the car from my folks' house, where the reception was. But we only drove around town for a little while to catch up with each other and take a few deep breaths and let everyone leave who was going to leave. Then we went back to my parents' house again, changed into our jeans, and had a wonderful relaxed visit with our folks, our sisters, and the rest of our friends who were still there. We wouldn't have missed that for anything.

Rice

If you have any control in advance over those who throw rice, suggest they don't. The tossing of grains on the newly married couple comes from times where fertility and fruitfulness meant everything. "May you have as many children as these grains of rice that rain down on you." High infant mortality is not what it once was, and the need for "many hands on the farm" is no longer relevant. Most hotels and churches flat out prohibit the practice. They do not appreciate rice, confetti, or birdseed all over the foyer, the walkways, the lobby, the carpets, the stairways. Especially on tiles and cement, it is a liability. Birdseed offers no advantages over rice and is just as messy and inaccessible to the birds. Remember, the birds aren't going to clean up after you. Some person who needs to be paid will clean up after you, and you will probably be charged some kind of rice fee. Churches often have services very shortly after your departure and need the place clean and swept. Beyond the hired help at the

---

IT WAS IN APRIL. We have this huge bush of tiny little fragrant pink roses in our yard which was blooming its head off! The smell was fabulous. So we decided to line these tiny little roses across the dashboard of their car—and outside along the windshield—on every little ledge we could find in the car. We tied a few streamers to their antenna. And when they came out to the driveway to get in the car, we were all there to wish them off and we showered them with rose petals. When they came back from their wedding trip, they said the car still had a fabulous smell of roses to it.

---

church, be sure you have left a contingent of helpers to get the place back in relative shape after you leave.

If you are in an outdoor place where grains of seed fall into the grass or pose no hazard to walking, by all means get sent off with the blessing of rice or seeds.

May your creative works be as numerous as these grains of seed, abundant your undertakings and the service you bring to this community.

3

Matters of Hospitality

Invitations

Your invitation reflects something of you, your combined styles and tastes, and the manner in which you want to enter this sacred union. The announcement you send invites your family and friends to join you in this moment. It asks them to bring their blessings and good wishes and their promise to stand by you for the rest of your days. Your text should reflect something of that spirit.

Who makes the announcement? In the past, the invitation was extended in the name of the people (usually the bride's parents) who were sponsoring the celebration. Today it is more fitting to mention both families. If you have been independent for some time or if you are marrying for the second (or third) time, you should send your invitations out using your own names.

————

After you have composed the text of your invitations, you will have to visit the printers. Although they will invariably show you the ready-made and metallic-embossed cards they have on hand, you can do much better by avoiding what often looks tinny or garish. If you want something to embellish your invitations, consider drawing something yourselves or having a gifted friend do something for you. One couple used a bird standing on a flower which a young nephew drew in his childlike way. Creamy papers or flecked recycled papers, printed or handwritten, all add a personal note.

Here are examples of invitations the two of you might use for inspiration or as models for your own invitations.

When one parent is a widow

Philip and Edwina McCarthy and Ester Connolly
invite you to participate in prayer and blessing at the
holy union of their children

ADRIENNE MARY MCCARTHY

and

BRENDAN JOSEPH CONNOLLY

Ten o'Clock A.M.
April Fifth, Nineteen Hundred Ninety-Nine

Church of the Holy Sepulcher

2349 Lake View Avenue

Chicago, Illinois

Multiple parents and stepparents

Leonard Kent ◆ Joanne Kent ◆ Maria Kent ◆ Fred Ellis ◆ Barbara Ellis

Martin Dosh ◆ Eleanor Dosh

Invite You to Celebrate the Marriage of their Children

KATHERINE KENT

and

SEAN ELLIS

14 September 1998

5:00 P.M.

CHURCH OF THE NATIVITY

1749 Grant Avenue

Tilwakau, Wisconsin

Reception following

Dosh Residence

145 High Bluff Drive

Oseguah, Wisconsin

Two-family hosts

Edward Theodore Behr and Ursula Ellen Behr

José Garcia Arango and Augustina Arango

cordially invite you to celebrate with them the marriage
of their children

ELLEN MARY BEHR

and

PEDRO ANTONIO ARANGO

Star of the Sea Church

440 Archer Avenue

Falcon, Texas

27 May, 1999

2:00 P.M.

Reception following at the church hall

Second marriage or independent couple not in a church

GERALDINE FAIBORN FAHLE *and* FRAZER MARK DICKMAN
and their families
invite you to celebrate their marriage

June the twenty-seventh, nineteen hundred and ninety-nine
Twelve Noon

Faludi House

1893 Lake Avenue

Grosse Pointe, Illinois

Reception Following

Informal outdoor wedding with potluck

Rejoice with us at the celebration of our marriage

KATE CHRISTINA KUZYK *and* GARY EDWARD LAKEN

June 14, 1999

The Bluffs
Foot of Nineteenth Street
Seaside, Georgia

Casual wear
Potluck following
Please bring a dish to share

Informal wedding with potluck

MARIKA RENATE JENSEN *and* ALLEN ROBERT MESSNER

Marriage Ceremony:
Christ in the Desert Episcopal Church
312 Sunrise Ridge Road
Bogan, Arizona
28 December, 1999
10:00 A.M.

Reception following
Sibley Hall

Setting aside a whole weekend for a wedding

CLAIRE METCALF *and* MICHAEL RADOCI
and their families
ask you to join them

in a weekend of celebration and blessing
for the occasion of their wedding
23–25 May 1999

Friday Evening: Dinner, music making, story telling
Grady Lake Lodge

Saturday Noon, Nuptial Mass
Church of St. Anthony

Dinner and Dancing following, Grady Lake Lodge

Sunday Morning 25, Festive Brunch, Grady Lake Lodge

Grady Lake Resort
County Road F
Grady Lake, Nevada

The Rehearsal

The wedding rehearsal has become an entity in its own right. It has two very important functions.

First, it serves a social function. It gathers families and other members of the family, introduces them to one another, and leads naturally into a dinner, where they will continue socializing.

It also makes the ceremony run more smoothly by giving everyone a chance to run through their part in it. When people know what they are supposed to do and find their place and position in the ceremony, the flow of the wedding is smoother, certain awkward issues are dealt with up front, there is no mystery about what will happen the next day, and everyone relaxes considerably. When people are at ease, they do a better job with their part in the ceremony and are able to enjoy it more. Their comfort level has a direct effect on the comfort of the guests.

Invite all the people who will have a role in the wedding: the presider, your witnesses, all the parents and stepparents, children if you have any, ushers, welcomers, readers, and musicians. If it's important for you to have the organist present, be sure to make arrangements beforehand (and be prepared to pay an additional fee). There is no need for the acolytes to be there unless they are members of the family or extended family. Stress the importance of beginning promptly and ending promptly.

Since you will have already discussed the details of the wedding with the presider, allow him or her to take the lead. (The rehearsal is not the time to discuss the ceremony's details with others.) You do not want to hold up the presider with idle issues if you have gone over these earlier.

The rehearsal should allow ample time for:

- *The readers to practice their readings from start to finish as if it were a dress rehearsal (which it is) with microphone and all*
- *The entire wedding party to understand their place and role in the procession and recession*
- *The ushers or greeters to understand their roles*
- *Members of the family to work out who will sit where*
- *The couple themselves and their witnesses to walk through the heart of the ceremony—the vows and exchange of rings*

AS A MINISTER, I have officiated at a few weddings in my day, but as far as I'm concerned, the rehearsal is the most thankless day I spend with the couple. Here's what happens: I give my Friday night to the bridal party for a rehearsal and they arrive late or in a party mood and they refuse to pay attention to my direction. The mother of the bride is sure to think she's in charge and insert herself and her wishes and complaints. She doesn't realize that this is not her wedding and that the couple has already made their own plans and choices. And if there's a wedding coordinator in attendance, she really tries my patience. She always has her own ideas which have more to do with the look of things than with the essence of things.

I SEE MY ROLE at the wedding rehearsal as particularly important. People have just arrived from all over the place. They are travel-worn and tired. They are excited and nervous. They are thrilled to see friends and relatives they haven't seen in ages. There are always the few who know no one else and have a hard time feeling a part of the group. There is the bride and the groom who feel at sixes and sevens because they are trying to juggle a lot of levels! Their own roles, the introduction of their friends and families. Often there are the tensions of divorced parents, which make a lot of electricity in the air. Without wasting any time I take the leadership. I gather everyone in a circle and let them introduce themselves around the ring, who they are, what their role is, where they came from. Once around the circle takes less time than the free-for-all that would otherwise take place. Then I ask them to hold hands, close their eyes, and I pray with them. I lower my voice. I purposely take them into a very quiet, reverent place. Then I invite them to stand there silently until hearts are calm. I never raise my voice again, but I do give out directions and give a running commentary on why we have chosen to do things in a certain way. I don't ever give the impression that we haven't got every facet of this rehearsal planned and finalized. This evening is not up for grabs. I find that if I can calm the group and make of them a cohesive lot, I not only get out of there faster, but they calm right down, knowing that someone is in charge, someone actually wants to help them do the best possible job, someone cares about how this wedding day will come off. The rehearsal sets the spiritual tone and that's my special contribution.

Notes to a Reader

When you ask your friends to read at your wedding, you will want to choose them not only because they are significant in your lives, but because they are good readers. Show them this chapter. It will give them the kind of coaching and information necessary for a successful delivery. This chapter is written for them.

It is an honor to be asked to read for a wedding, and you will want to do the very best job you can. Below is a description of your role, some suggestions for how to prepare, and encouragement to lower any anxiety you might have.

Attitude

As a reader you perform a service but do not give a performance. There's a difference. When you read a passage of Scripture (or even a nonscriptural piece) at a wedding, you will use some of the same skills actors and professional speakers use. You vary your pitch, your volume, your tempo. You pause for dramatic effect, to evoke feeling and convey meaning. You will not do so to entertain or call attention to yourself, but to serve a community engaged in a sacred action. As a reader of Scripture, you will be speaking God's word.

There is a story of a dinner party held in England following the Second World War, attended by a famous actor. After the meal he was persuaded, with very little encouragement, to perform soliloquies from various plays. At one point, when guests were asking him to perform their favorite pieces, a priest, an older man, asked him to recite the Twenty-third Psalm, "The Lord is my shepherd." He did so, and everyone applauded. Then the actor turned to the priest and asked him to recite the same psalm. The priest complied, and when he finished everyone fell silent—in awe. At last the actor observed, "I recited it as if I knew the psalm. You, as if you know the shepherd."

You don't have to give the most powerful or professional rendition of your passage. Rather, allow others to hear and experience God's word in all its depth and layers of meaning. Don't assume a pious, solemn, or artificially "holy" voice, because what is not authentic becomes a distraction. Speak in your normal voice and with the rhythm that comes to you naturally. Especially if your text is a sacred text, focus on serving God, whose word you dare to speak, and attend to this gathered community, who longs to be touched with meaning.

When people thank you afterward for helping them hear the reading in a way that truly moved them, you will know you succeeded.

Nervousness

If the thought of reading to a large group of people makes you anxious, you can do three things so your anxiety does not defeat you.

Use your fear as an incentive to practice. If you think you can stand up in front of others to read a passage without being adequately prepared, you should be nervous! But if you are ready and know what you're about, you will also feel confident.

Use your fear as a source of energy. A little nervousness is a good thing; it gives you a spark of energy to put into the reading.

Focus on the people who are listening. By paying attention to your listeners, you will become less self-conscious and therefore less nervous. You will know how you are doing by reading the faces of the people. Do the people in the back of the church look like they can hear? Are all eyes forward? Hang your ego on the nearest peg and focus on this group. "Love the listeners" and your self-consciousness will melt away.

Preparation

Study the passage. Read it to yourself over and over again. Look up unfamiliar words. Ask about the meaning of unfamiliar concepts. Read the surrounding context of the passage.

Understand the meaning of the passage. If someone asked you to summarize the passage in your own words, what would you say?

Attend to the feelings conveyed by the passage. How does the passage make you feel as you read it? What feelings are being expressed in the passage itself? How do you want the listeners to feel as they hear you proclaim it?

Determine the passage's attitude. Does it mean to instruct, to admonish, or to encourage? Does the writer sound like a wise teacher, a worried parent, or a caring friend?

Print out the passage. You may want to prepare your own copy of the reading in large type and dark print so that you can easily see it. Capitalize or underline words or phrases that you want to emphasize. Put a slash at the end of a sentence or section to remind yourself where to pause. You can practice with it and then slip it into the book you will be reading from.

Rehearsal

Before the formal rehearsal at the church, rehearse your reading aloud.

Add variety to your voice. Emphasize a word or sentence by changing your volume. Speak loudly where you want to lend a sense of importance. Speak softly (as long as you can still be heard) and people will lean forward to pay attention. Altering your pitch conveys different feelings: A high pitch indicates joy or excitement, a lower pitch conveys a sense of solemnity or foreboding. With practice you can avoid speaking either in a monotone or a singsong voice.

Pay attention to the tempo of your speech. Inexperienced or nervous readers often speak too quickly, as if rushing to get through with it. Read at about the same rate as you normally speak. Change the tempo to add variety, mood, and a sense of movement.

Pause when appropriate. A pause invites listeners to anticipate what you are about to say or gives them time to reflect on what you just said.

Church Rehearsal

At the rehearsal itself, have a copy of your reading with you. Take the opportunity to practice your reading as you will present it at the wedding. If you are going to read from a podium using a microphone during the service, practice approaching the podium and standing in it. Know how to turn on the reading light or switch on the microphone. Be sure to read your passage at least once using the microphone. Ask people in the back of the church if they can easily hear you.

Ready. Set. Go.

Ready. Did you slip your marked copy of the reading into the book at the podium? No one should see your paper as you read. Your reading should flow as from the book.

Set. During the service, as you are waiting for your time to read, you may find yourself getting anxious. Take a few deep breaths, and as you exhale, allow yourself to relax. Remind your-self that you are not the focus of the wedding or even of the reading. Everyone is on your side and will overlook your mis-takes. Pray that this service you render will be for the good of all who hear it.

Go. When it comes time to read, walk confidently forward. If the church prominently features an altar (as in a Roman Catholic, Episcopalian, or Lutheran church), pause in front of it and bow your head slightly in its direction. Walk to the podium, find your reading in the book, and adjust the microphone so it points directly toward your mouth. Take a moment. Look at the people you are addressing and give them time to stop shuffling and look toward you. If you are reading an introduction that ex-plains the passage, read it and then pause. Now begin the passage with "A reading from . . ." Then *proclaim* your passage. If your reading was a scriptural passage, pause briefly at the end and con-clude with the words: "The Word of the Lord." Wait for the people to respond: "Thanks be to God." Now return to your seat. Be glad that you were a conduit for the Spirit speaking through Sacred Scripture.

A Note on Reading at Outdoor Weddings

If the wedding is planned for outdoors, in a park or garden, the same guidelines above apply—with two cautions.

First, it is very difficult to make yourself heard in an open-air setting. Unless you present your reading to a small group of peo-ple who are gathered close together, you will need a micro-phone. Ask for one to be set up. Unless you are a formally trained speaker or a professional actor, you will not be able to make yourself heard.

Remember, an outdoor wedding may mix two different levels: It is religious (there may be a minister, prayers, and vows), but is not in a church. For that reason, you will need to bring an extra measure of dignity and meaning to your presentation. By your manner and spirit you will set a tone, state a belief, evoke a feeling.

A Note on Nonbiblical Readings

Whether the wedding takes place inside a church or not, you may be asked to present a reading from a source other than the Bible. A poem, perhaps, or a famous writer's reflection on the nature of love. Again, the same guidelines apply—with, again, a caution.

You have to work harder to convey the passage's meaning, since your listeners will probably be unfamiliar with it. Quite often people know the Scripture passages read at weddings and have some familiarity with biblical style. That makes it easier to hear and understand the reading. It is more difficult to understand a passage that is completely new to them—especially if it is poetry. Only when you understand the passage yourself—its meaning and development—can you hope to get the reading across to the listeners.

We know you can do it! Good luck!

The Printed Program

You may decide to produce a booklet that outlines the order of service so your guests can follow along. In it you can print the responses and the text and music of any hymns you might want the people to sing together. While such a booklet is in no way a requirement, it can help your guests know where they are and what comes next. Think of it as a device that allows people to participate more fully in the ceremony. It should not distract them from the central action.

It is best *not* to print the texts to the readings themselves in the program, since people will read the text along with your reader instead of looking up, sitting back, and listening to the words. Offer, instead, the sources and titles of your readings so people can find them again later if they want to. For the same reason, you do not want to print the vows. If you reproduce texts and music that are not part of the public domain, you will need to respect the copyright laws. (Your musicians can help you.)

This booklet is not a program, complete with the cast of characters in order of appearance, like the one you might receive at the theater. A wedding is both serious and sacred, and you don't want anything to imply that it is merely a performance.

Below, you will find samples of various orders of worship with degrees of formality.

Sample for a Church Wedding

Suggestion: Along with your names and the date of your wedding, you may wish to put a quotation on the front cover as part of your design.

Celebrating the Marriage of

CLAIRE MARY ALLISON *and* JACKSON R. BRAGG

Where there is charity and love,
there is God.
The love of God
has gathered us together.
Let us rejoice in God
and be glad.

18 August 1999

Second page:

PRELUDE

Jesu, Joy of Man's Desiring J. S. Bach

Canon in D Major J. Pachelbel

PROCESSIONAL "Joyful Joyful We Adore Thee"

Beethoven

LITURGY OF THE WORD

Reading 1: Genesis 2:18–24

RESPONSORIAL PSALM The Lord Is Kind and Merciful

SECOND READING I Corinthians 12:31–13:8a

ALLELUIA Sung by All

GOSPEL John 15:12–16

HOMILY

Third page:

RITE OF MARRIAGE

VOWS

BLESSING OF RINGS

PRAYERS OF THE PEOPLE

THE LORD'S PRAYER

KISS OF PEACE Wedding Song

Heinrich Schütz

NUPTIAL BLESSING

RECESSIONAL Trumpet Voluntary

Purcell/Clarke

The Back Cover:

PRESIDER: The Reverend Merideth Foley-Owens

PARENTS: Mary and Nestor Allison ◆

Nanette and Bill Bragg

WITNESSES: Claude Allison ◆ Luellen Bragg Ofuji

HOSTS AND USHERS: Betsy and Parker Allison and

Jennifer Bragg, Joseph Kalenkiewicz,

Cindy Bragg Hecker, David Dover and

Lizbet Hecker

READERS: Dorothy Forde, Grandmother of the

Bride

Ted Evans, Godfather of the Groom

MUSICIANS: Cantor, Rose Schmitz

Organist, Jean-Pierre Garnier

Trumpets, Marcella and Jackson

Bettencort

Sample for a Church Ceremony
Within the Context of the Eucharist

Suggestion: Along with your names and the date of your wedding, you may wish to put a quotation on the front cover as part of your design.

The Nuptial Mass

of

MARY ELLEN KENNER

and

PAUL EDWARD COLE

September 22, 1998

I will betroth you to myself forever,
Betroth you with integrity and justice
with tenderness and love

I will betroth you to myself with faithfulness
And you will come to know God.
Hosea 2:19-22

Second page

Suggestion: You can list the pieces of music being played and their composers. Pieces to be sung in unison might have page references for a hymnal or song book already placed in the seats.

PRELUDE

Gather Us In   Haugen

Set Me as a Seal   Clausen

PROCESSIONAL Trumpet Processional

Campra

GREETING AND OPENING PRAYERS

FIRST READING Jeremiah 31:31–32a, 33–34a

RESPONSORIAL PSALM Psalm 118

Marty Haugen

Refrain: This is the day the Lord has made.

Let us rejoice and be glad.

This is the day the Lord has made.

Let us rejoice and be glad.

SECOND READING Colossians 3:12–17

GOSPEL ACCLAMATION Alleluia

Marty Haugen

GOSPEL John 15:12–16

HOMILY

Suggestion: The third page might begin with the marriage rites.

MARRIAGE RITE AND EXCHANGE OF VOWS

BLESSING AND EXCHANGE OF RINGS

PREPARATION OF GIFTS "The Servant Song"
Richard Gillard

EUCHARISTIC ACCLAMATION

THE LORD'S PRAYER

PASSING THE KISS OF PEACE

COMMUNION SONG "Come to the Water"
John Foley, S.J.

MEDITATION "Wedding Hymn"
G. F. Handel

PRAYER OF THE COUPLE "Magnificat of Betrothal"
Johnson

RECESSIONAL "Alleluia, Sing!"
David Haas

Suggestion: On the back cover and away from the context of the ceremony you may list the people who have special roles in the ceremony.

PRESIDER: The Rev. Edward H. Doyle

PARENTS: Helen and Hugh Kenner ◆
Jane and Max Cole

WITNESSES: Judith Kenner ◆ Mathew Cole

HOSTS AND USHERS: Linda, Peter, and Jeffry Kenner
Daniel and Abby Cole and
David Cotter

READERS: Marissa Dobson–Carey, Godmother of
the Bride
Michael Cole, Grandfather of the
Groom

PRESENTATION OF THE GIFTS: Mattias Gruber, Njoki Ruminjo,
Liz Chang

MUSICIANS: Ellen Leffison, Cantor

Robert Thomas, Organist

Willy Voorst-Peeters, Violin

Sample for an Informal Wedding in Nature

The format for this was a rolled scroll, that is, everything was on a single sheet of paper.

The Marriage of

SUSANNA BICKERSTAFF *and* CARL PACKI

Mariposa Meadows. California Sierras

April 22, 2000

Your hands lie open in the long fresh grass,
The finger-points look through like rosy blooms;
Your eyes smile peace. The pasture gleams and glooms
'Neath billowing skies that scatter and amass.
All round our nest, far as the eye can pass,
Are golden kingcup-fields with silver edge
Where the cow-parsley skirts the hawthorn-hedge.
'Tis visible silence, still as the hour-glass.

Deep in the sun-searched growths the dragonfly
Hangs like a blue thread loosened from the sky:
So this winged hour is dropt to us from above.
Oh! clasp we to our hearts, for deathless dower,
This close-companioned inarticulate hour
When twofold silence was the song of love.

DANTE GABRIEL ROSSETTI

A Processional with Bride and Groom:
Susanna and Carl

and Their Families:
Adelle and Dennis Browning, Randall Bickerstaff,
Jenny, Jason and Jessica Bickerstaff
Angela Packi, Jim and Ginger Packi,
Laura and Maurice Palmer-Packi

and Witnesses
Andrea Baudis and Martin Gerwig

Sheep May Safely Graze J. S. Bach

Concerto in A minor G. P. Telemann

Recorders: Adelle, Jenny, and Jessica
Violas da Gamba: Jason and Fred Pai

Welcome and Invocation
Reverend Althea Oxberry

Readings I
Selections from Emily Dickinson, Rilke, and Shakespeare
Performing artists: Rose Overturf and Owen Newton

Readings II
Selections from Song of Songs, I Corinthians, Psalm 23
Readers: Florence Nicosia, Jim Packi, and Sigrid Swenson

Gospel
John 15:12-16
Althea Oxberry

Circling the Bride and Groom
Each person brings a flower to the basket,
pronounces a blessing on the rings,
forms a circle around the couple.

The Exchange of Vows

The Exchange of Rings
THE BLESSING

THE KISS
SIX DANCES OF THE RENAISSANCE, M. Praetorius
Guests will find baskets with instruments:
small kettledrums, hand drums, bells, tambourines,
a triangle, wood blocks, and cymbals.
Catch the rhythm and join in the circle dance.

Musicians:
Piccolo and soprano recorder: Hans Linden
Tenor recorder and alto recorder: Elizabeth Wilke
Lute and guitar: Walt and Netty Baudis
Soprano recorders: Adelle, Jenny, and Jessica
Violas da gamba: Jason and Fred Pai

Some people use appropriate clip-art to embellish the cover, have everything written in calligraphy, or ask an artist to design the whole booklet. Some people write a greeting and note of gratitude to their parents, which seems more the sort of thing you would do for them privately (say, in a warm letter written together on your wedding trip). Others write greetings and thanks to their guests, both of which seem redundant, since you will be greeting and thanking them throughout the day. When the church or site of the wedding is widely separated from the reception site, some people include a hand-drawn map on the back cover to help the guests find their way.

We offer these examples of printed orders for a wedding service not as prototypes either for their content or format, but only to stir your own imaginations and to encourage you to use your good taste and discretion.

4

Making a Marriage

Marriage Preparation

It takes a lifetime to prepare for marriage. All the experiences we have had until the point of marriage have, in fact, contributed to who we are. The people who were important to us in our growing up, especially our parents, made a deep and lasting imprint on us. And for better or for worse we learned from them how to relate—learned the very workings of a marriage. Consciously and unconsciously the relationships we formed with others—our family members, our friends, the persons we dated—were the practice fields of our learning about love and commitment, disagreements and disappointments. Looking back on that field, we get our sense of what a life-long relationship might look like.

And yet for all that, marriage is still unlike any other relationship we have had. Because of the commitment marriage asks, it demands special attention right from the start.

Every marriage deserves to set out on a firm footing. For this reason there are many opportunities available to help prepare for marriage—more opportunities than ever before in history. And more than ever before in history, we need to seek out these opportunities and get them to work for us.

Three basic forms of premarriage preparation are available to anyone hoping to marry. There is the counseling provided by the priest or minister who will also perform your ceremony. The priest or minister meets with the couple on several occasions to address the questions and relationship issues that are best covered before entering marriage. Many churches require the couple to take a computer-scored inventory—one is called Prepare/Enrich—which assesses their attitudes about the main issues of married life. The results of the survey are then the topics for discussion.

WHY IS IT we allow these kids to drift into marriage trailing rosy clouds of romantic feeling? We shove them off with solemn ceremonies on a joint enterprise fraught with complexity and have made no serious effort to enlighten them! The dreary statistics suggest a substantial number of these marriages are doomed to fail. Would serious scientists keep making the same experiment without tallying the conclusions or changing their methods?

WOULD YOU LET a twenty-two-year-old determine the course of the rest of your life?

Second, there are marriage preparation programs offered through local or regional churches. The programs may extend over several evenings or a weekend. They are usually well structured and may be led by an experienced team of married couples and clergy. The Roman Catholic church in most dioceses offers programs called Pre-Cana, Evenings for the Engaged, and Engaged Encounter. Lutherans offer Lutheran Engaged Encounter.

BOTH MY FIANCÉE and I are practicing M.D.'s. There's been a little water under the bridge. So, given our age and experience, I was put off that the priest wanted us to spend a weekend with a program called Engaged Encounter before he'd witness our marriage. We figured we'd be thrown in with a lot of dreamy kids with questionable IQs—and we'd be trapped there overnight! I have to tell you, we were both more than pleasantly surprised. It was the first time we had that much time just talking about us, our hopes and fears. We really took the time to delve into some of the things we'd never taken time for before. The experience was very important and helpful to us. We'd recommend it to everyone.

And finally, a growing number of professional therapists offer premarriage counseling.

Most marriage preparation programs use a combination of approaches: educational, experiential exercises, surveys, written exercises, and many opportunities for discussion. They begin by helping couples explore what each person brings to the relationship. Through presentations and discussions they help couples reflect on the factors that influence the stability and quality of marriage and give suggestions and practical resources tailored to strengthening each particular marriage.

Most marriage preparation programs address a variety of issues: family—including family of origin, extended, and blended families—finances, children and child-rearing, faith and religion, sex, communication styles—including rules for fair fighting and making up—and personality types. Once over lightly, we touch on some of these issues below. Read the questions we pose, pay attention not just to the answers you give but to the way you go about sharing your answers with each other. Watch for feelings and the quality of your listening skills. Watch how you discuss what is difficult and where you want to avoid, deflect, or interrupt.

Family

The family we were born into establishes our conscious and unconscious model of marriage. From them we learn what to expect of marriage and how to approach it. That could be healthy. That could be less than healthy. No family is perfect and no family is perfectly dreadful. But when we are ready to strike out on our own, we need to look at the way our families formed us.

What is your family like?

Who do you call family? Parents, stepparents, brothers and sisters, aunts, uncles, cousins, and grandparents?

What was/is your parents' relationship like? Loving? Openly affectionate? Consistent? Equal? Respectful? Stressful? Combative? How did your parents handle conflict? What was/is their way of resolving it?

If your parents were divorced, how did that affect you?

What did your experience of growing up in your family teach

you about marriage, about what's important in forming and maintaining a healthy relationship?

What about your parents' relationship do you want to emulate? What would you do differently?

How do you interact with your future in-laws? Do they approve of you? Like you?

Do your parents approve of your choice?

Will you expect to celebrate your holidays with family? Which family? Where? On your own as a couple?

Which family's traditions do you plan on using when you celebrate?

Finances

Studies reveal that finances—and disputes over them—play a major role in undermining marriages.

What do you currently earn?

What debts (including credit card debts) do you owe?

Are you a spender or a saver?

How do you budget your expenses?

Do you have a savings plan for retirement?

Do you plan on keeping your money in a joint account or in separate accounts? Why?

Who will handle paying the bills and balancing the checkbook?

How will you go about making financial decisions?

Children and Child Rearing

You need a license to drive a car, buy a gun, and get married—goes the old saw—but no one needs a license to have children. *Becoming* a parent isn't hard! It's *being* a parent that is.

If you have children from a previous marriage, how will they be incorporated into your new life together? What role will the stepparent play in raising them and, especially, in disciplining them?

If you don't have children, do you plan on having any? How many would you like? When do you plan on having them? If, for some reason, you can't have children, what would you do?

What kind of parents do you think you will be?

What is important that you want to pass on to your children?

What have you learned about being a parent from your parents that you want to emulate? What attitudes and ideas don't you want to pass on to your children?

What do you think a father's role is?

A mother's role?

The role of grandparents?

How do you think those roles support one another? Complement one another? Conflict with one another?

If both of you are keeping your last names or hyphenating them, which surname will you give your children?

Faith and Religion

A shared religious faith is a "predictor of marital success" say most sociological studies.

What was your experience of religion as you grew up?

What part, if any, does it play in your lives now?

What spiritual values are important to you?

What do you believe about God? About the purpose of life? About morality, forgiveness, and death?

How serious are you about living your religious beliefs?

What if you have different beliefs?

Do you think differences in religious beliefs and understandings would put limits on how solid your marriage can be? Why?

What faith or participation in church or a religious community do you hope to pass on to your children?

How important is it for you to worship together?

How will you celebrate religious holidays? Whose family traditions will you follow? Whose religious traditions?

Sex

Sex isn't just the mechanics of lovemaking. Our sexuality is a basic part of who we are, how we express ourselves, and the way we relate intimately with the person we love. Sexual difficulties may reflect other, sometimes hidden, relational problems, and can in turn add additional stresses to the marriage. But sexual intimacy and mutuality can also be a means of healing and wholesomeness, of relational strengthening and joy.

What is the nature of your sexual relationship at this stage?

How satisfied are you? What aspects of your sexual relationship do you think the two of you need to discuss in greater detail?

What can you do to keep your lovemaking fresh and alive?

How do you think sex will change with time as your relationship deepens?

How much physical closeness do you desire?

How comfortable are you talking about sex and your sexual feelings and desires?

How do you feel about your partner's sexual history?

Communication Styles

Communication is more than talking and listening. It's about *how* we talk to each other and the quality of our listening, what we say with the tone of our voice, the expression on our faces, the look in our eyes. It's about asking questions and paying attention to the answers, listening for what gets left unspoken and for the feelings and intentions behind the words. Communication is reading the other's eyes and body language and eliciting gently what the other might be afraid to say. Communication is letting the other know what lies deepest in us and not being afraid to expose ourselves. Communication is reflecting back what we hear until we both agree we understand. Communication is about honesty and the way we express it or accept it.

What do you like most about the way your partner listens to you?

When is the last time you and your partner talked about what you like most about each other?

What subjects can't you talk about?

What subjects are you afraid to bring up?

Do you ever fight?

Do you tend to bear grudges?

Do you spill your feelings or withhold them?

When you disagree with each other or get angry with each

other, how does that make you feel? What do you feel like doing? Running away, literally? Shouting? Withdrawing psychologically?

RULES FOR FAIR FIGHTING

HAD A FIGHT LATELY? Sooner or later you will. And that's no cause for alarm. Disagreements and conflicts are an inevitable part of any intimate relationship. They may even be necessary to growing, sharing yourselves, and bonding as a couple. What's most important is *how* you address and resolve the problems that come up. Here are some suggestions.

1. Pick the right time for an argument, preferably when both of you are rested and not hungry and when you have enough time to adequately address the issue.
2. Stick to one subject.
3. Don't bring up past hurts.
4. Choose the right place for your fight. Some couples make it a point never to fight in the bedroom. They want to keep it a place associated with love and intimacy. Don't argue in front of other people or in public places.
5. Choose your words carefully. Avoid saying *always* and *never*. Calling each other names or using obscenities also ends most arguments (without finishing them) and leaves a nasty feeling in the air.
6. Use "I" statements, sharing your own feelings and opinions. Don't say, "How like you! You're always late! You're so bloody inconsiderate, you never think about anyone but yourself." Say, instead, "When you're late, I get worried and angry."

7. Don't hit below the belt. Lovers know each other's greatest vulnerabilities: The things their partners dislike about themselves—like issues of weight, appearance, or sexuality. Even if you apologize later for saying something hostile about the other person, you have destroyed something deep in the other person's self-confidence or trust. That's something very hard to heal, if it ever heals at all.

8. Finish the argument, if at all possible. Don't leave unresolved conflicts and feelings for a later fight.

How do you resolve the issue? Or do you keep arguing about the same thing?

Do you cry easily or use tears to avoid conflict?

Do you give in easily or stubbornly "stand on principles"?

Do you tend to store up the things that hurt or offend you and then use them all at once as ammunition?

Can you admit that you're wrong and ask for forgiveness? Can you forgive?

What are you like when you are sick? Do you like to be looked after or left alone?

What are you like when you have to look after someone who is sick? Are you a relatively healthy person? Do you have more than your share of physical concerns?

Do you ask for what you need? Or do you want the other to guess?

How do you feel about your work? Do you see it as permanent? How do you get along with your coworkers? Do you bring work or worries home with you? Do you want to listen to your partner's concerns about work?

Personality Styles

Our personalities are a composite of traits. Some we inherited from our parents. Some are attitudes and habits we learned from others or refined on our own. Add to that mix the conscious and unconscious memories, feelings, and thought patterns that seem to be part of our blood and bone. Who we are—our basic personality—changes very little over the course of our lives.

Are you pessimistic or optimistic? Outgoing or shy? A morning person or a late-night person? Neat or messy? Punctual or

---

I FELL IN LOVE with his quirky idiosyncrasies, his innocence, the slightly bewildered, flustered, gone-last-week air he had about him. I found it utterly endearing and it made me want to take care of him. Now I wonder! Today those are the very qualities that drive me flat-out bonkers.

MY DEAR LOVE is a gadget freak. Part of me finds it amusing. But sometimes it worries me. On Saturday he goes to the hardware store and almost salivates over tire gauges, bins of hinges, sets of wrenches all lined up according to size, a screwdriver that can do everything but play the piano. I can handle all that. But then come the big-ticket items. Office gadgets. Camping equipment. Rock-climbing equipment. And now a sailboat. I accuse him of falling in love with these items. To convince me how necessary this piece is, he conjures up images of how the two of us are going to love having this whatever—and he hauls it to his place, and it just sits there. The love affair lasts maybe a week. How many of these mistresses can he accommodate over time? What's his fascination going to do to our budget once we marry? How long am I going to find this funny?

---

habitually late? A romantic or hard-nosed realist? Emotionally expressive or reserved? Impulsive or disciplined? Spontaneous or organized?

What's your idea of a good time? Going to a movie or staying home? Hiking or reading a book? Throwing a party or entertaining another couple at home?

Do you come to decisions quickly without second-guessing yourself, or do you agonize over every possible alternative?

Are you emotional or intellectual?

After You Are Married

It is unrealistic, of course, to resolve every problem before you get married, but you owe it to yourselves to address as many im-

---

RANT MODE ON: There is no such thing as an issue too trivial to be the focus of serious marital dispute and pain. The color of the socks I wore was a focus of great frustration for my wife for many years. Of course it was not the socks; it was a whole constellation of stuff beginning with attitudes about other people's opinions of one's dress and demeanor, her unsatisfactory relations with her parents (which got lived out again in her relations with me), beliefs about what she could and could not take the initiative about in our relationship, and probably deeper layers too. But the socks focused it and took the heat because they were safer and more external than the real issues. And I fought back with a vehemence better reserved for life-and-death issues, probably for reasons having to do with my personality, family experience, and weak sense of self. Would premarital sock-choice discussions have solved the problems? No, but discussion might have gotten us faster to a place where the real issues could be dealt with constructively. End of rant.

---

portant ones as you can. There will always be surprises up ahead, and that's one of the mysteries of love. Mysteries? Yes. Secrets? No. Marriage preparation should surface anything that might be an impediment to your relationship. If one of you, for example, adamantly refuses to have children and the other wants two or three, talk about it. Resolve the issue before you agree to marry. The so-called smaller issues can take on a life of their own and you will need to address them bravely and deeply in order to grow.

JUST ABOUT EVERY YEAR my husband and I make a guided, private retreat together, take a course, or arrange a few visits with our favorite counselor. Early in our marriage we promised each other we'd do that. We see it like spring house-cleaning. Maintenance! It's not fun, no. But it *really* has helped us through a few rough spots. We appreciate that third person's input.

MARRIAGE IS A SACRAMENT that we keep on conferring on each other. It didn't just happen once, on our wedding day, but it has to happen every day with our conscious effort, love, selflessness, and prayer.

Every year on our anniversary we gave each other this gift: I wrote a poem for my husband and my husband wrote me a letter. These writings often contained an overview of our experiences and relationship in the year that just passed. We were not much accomplished as writers, but the gift was more than money could buy— and we often didn't have money. I've kept all these things in a folder. After sixty-three years of marriage, my husband died. I took out the folder, and for the first time I read straight through all the pages we had there and found a history and review that went right from our innocent youth, through the war, our emigration, our six children. There were hard, very hard times. You can see it written there. All of it. My granddaughter wants to have a copy of it—but—I don't know. Would she understand it? If she could just understand that every marriage must leave place in it for God. Otherwise, there is no surviving, no growing.

Seek Out Models

Whether we plan it or not, we all have our heroes and the people who are models for us in certain areas of our lives. Why not go about this consciously and selectively? In time, you may want to attach yourselves to an older, successfully married couple. Marriage preparation programs have begun to actively encourage such relationships. An older couple, by word and example, by wisdom or experience, may model for you more about being married than all the other programs combined.

During the first few years of a marriage, the most struggles occur, the most adjustments are made, and the most habits—good or bad—are formed. Working to make a good marriage will always expose problems, especially at the start. No need to consider it a failure on your part or a sign of immaturity to seek outside help. On the contrary! To think you can do it all alone is often unrealistic. Approach the clergyperson who performed your ceremony and ask for guidance. Or visit a counselor together. Better to seek help sooner than later.

Those Doubts and Jitters

Of the most unwelcome spirits waiting at the threshold of a marriage are the nagging voices of doubt we sometimes call "the jitters."

As the wedding draws near and the reality of marriage becomes increasingly undeniable, you may find yourselves growing nervous. Not just about the wedding day, but about marriage itself. Even the most confidently in love, the most reasonable, the most even-tempered people admit to finding themselves easily agitated and short-tempered as the day approaches. Seems understandable.

Questions you thought you had answered long ago resurface

with a nagging intensity: Are you *really* ready to make a lifelong commitment and settle down? How do you know, absolutely positively, that you're making the right decision? Will your differences enrich your relationship over time, or will you get on each other's nerves with each passing year? Are the compromises you inevitably have to make too great for your peace of mind? If you were in love before—even married before—and the relationship turned sour, what makes you think this relationship will be better? Perhaps your financial considerations loom larger? Then questions resurface of children, of juggling two careers, of future in-laws, differing religions, disparate cultural backgrounds. . . . This family of spirits is an irritating lot.

Like the other spirits that lurk at the threshold of marriage, the jitters will either bless you or plague you, depending on how you handle them. If you stop to acknowledge them, they will serve you well. They will shake you up—sometimes literally waking you in the night—to demand your attention. But they will offer you valuable insights into yourselves and your relationship, insights that you might otherwise overlook. They will keep you from complacency until you face all your feelings, the ones of shame or fear or inadequacy as well as the feelings of joy and peace. But if you try to ignore the jitters—if you push them out of your awareness, pretending nothing is the matter—they will certainly haunt you. They will make you testy and irritable. They will descend on you with dark moods, with confusion, ambivalence, and impatience. They will interfere with your sleep and your appetite. And the reasons for their nattering will only be postponed for a less opportune or welcome situation.

Approach your jitters, then, as an invitation from your deepest self, the part that intuitively grasps a truth before you can reasonably explain it. Respect your intuition. The jitters ask you to take a hard and honest look at yourselves and this relationship. They ask you to pay full attention to your fears, your hunches, and even to your nighttime dreams.

Know that having the jitters does not mean that something is wrong with you or wrong with your relationship. These feelings don't invalidate your love, your relationship, or your decision to marry. More commonly they mean there is something within you or between you that the two of you still need to address. Bring your feelings to each other. Honestly sharing your nervousness and carefully respecting the other person's feelings are a sign of maturity and of your serious approach to marriage.

———

Begin by seeking out peace and a way to relax. Most of us benefit from taking quiet time by ourselves. In the flurry of wedding plans, you need periods of time to be alone with your thoughts. Get plenty of rest and exercise. Take a walk in a favorite place. Go to the park, the beach, the forest. Visit a museum. Work on your car. Putter in your garden. Browse in a bookstore. Practice yoga or play the piano. Do the things you have always enjoyed that absorb your attention, clear your mind, and help you relax. Set aside your concern until you feel yourself letting go and becoming less scattered. Remember, you are a person with a good and loving heart. Now, write out or ask yourself the questions that deserve your attention. Listen to what you hear yourself saying.

It is always a good thing to talk to each other about your concerns, but begin by relaxing and enjoying each other first. Go out on a real date together—to dinner perhaps—and make a promise not to talk about wedding plans for the duration of the meal. Delight in each other's company and remember how much you love each other. Then, when you feel reconnected, talk about your apprehensions and reservations. You may find that talking things over in a calm environment will deepen your mutual trust and bring you closer together.

If talking to each other doesn't resolve your worries or makes them worse—if you find that your concerns only rattle your partner—talk to someone else. Either of you individually may want to talk with someone who takes you seriously. Or you may want to go together to a professional—to the person who will be performing your ceremony or a therapist.

And finally, while prayer is no substitute for talking things through with other people, talking to God can help. Sit still. Pour out your heart to the Spirit who loves you and wants only the best for you. And listen. Your answer won't be written in the skies. Wait, rather, for wisdom and a deep sense of acceptance and peace.

More Than Mere Jitters

If talking and praying doesn't bring you relief or a sense of peace, your feelings may be more serious than a mere case of the jitters. Then it is important to look for three "red flags" that mark the source of greater concerns.

First, if you are unable or unwilling to talk to each other about your problem, that is a problem.

Second, if you expect a problem—any problem—to go away or fix itself after you marry—simply *because* you are married— you are setting yourself up for a fall. Marriage does indeed change some things, but it doesn't resolve basic problems in personality or relationship. It doesn't change character traits, improve behaviors, or obliterate old habits. If the two of you argue even now without coming to an agreement about budgets, for instance, or spending, credit card use, etc.—that isn't likely to change after your wedding. If one of you is bothered by something the other person *does*—flirting, drinking, taking potshots at your family, being late—or, more important, by something the other person *is*—passive or controlling, boisterous or bookish, introverted or party-loving—you have to realize that some habits should be dealt with now and some personality traits will likely never change.

Finally, if doubts or misgivings about your approaching mar-

I SHOULD HAVE KNOWN it wouldn't work. There were clues! Times before we married when I noticed his occasional angry outburst. Most of the time he was so romantic and kind. But every once in a great while he'd explode and I never could figure out what odd "infraction" of mine set him off. Eventually it terrified me. He'd begin by trying to look controlled, but he'd set his jaw and then he'd start yelling and shouting. Sometimes he'd throw something—a shoe, a book. Or he'd storm out of the house, slamming the door and roaring out of the driveway. He could barely talk to me for a day or two. And then, suddenly, everything would be just dandy again and he'd be so affectionate. It made me want to forget completely what had happened only days before. He had these two sides and I couldn't fit them together, like a Jekyll and Hyde. Sometimes I wanted to talk to him about those peculiar outbursts, but it was too scary—way too dangerous for me. Any question might be seen as a confrontation. I was always afraid I might touch off another one of his rages.

AS MY FELLOW marriage counselors will tell you, a very common mistake engaged couples make—and the most disastrous one—is thinking that marriage is a magic wand that will make a problem go away. People say old age makes people themselves, only more so. Well, the same is true for marriage. Marriage makes two people the couple they've always been, only more so. If there is love and empathy, acceptance and a gentle humor, if there is parity and mutual admiration before the wedding, all the better. But if from the beginning there is some basic miscommunication—if there are hurt feelings, secrets, niggling resentments, addictions, or personality traits they really don't like about the other person, marriage will not resolve this; it will make matters much worse.

riage arise early in your engagement and persist, they should be a cause for concern. Even though last-minute fears—even out-and-out panic—can be expected, doubts, hesitations, and reservations of long standing are more serious.

People who are divorced will tell you—*now*—they sensed from the beginning that their marriage was a mistake. Despite their nagging intuitions, they didn't know how to call the wedding off. Or didn't have the courage to turn back. Or couldn't find a rational explanation for their feelings. Or thought turning back would be too humiliating. Or felt pressed to continue because the wheels were rolling, their parents and friends were excited, and everyone was already deeply involved.

Problems won't go away by magic. If you are aware of a significant problem, you will perform a noble act for yourselves by calling off the wedding or postponing it until all the issues have been properly dealt with.

The jitters hover around the threshold. If you ignore them,

SHE STOOD AT THE BACK of the church, hanging on to her dad's arm. All through her engagement she had been making the major decisions and her fiancé was happily, obliviously passive. There was something about him that was charming enough, but he was also distant, disengaged, self-centered, very subtly manipulative. The bride struggled with massive attacks of doubt, confusion, foreboding, but tried to brush them off as "normal jitters." Her family had become painfully aware that something was off. "I didn't have to leave any hints about my feelings for my family to pick up. I slipped into really nasty moods! Everyone in the family was wrong and I was always making *excuses* for this man."

Her parents tried to respect their daughter's choice, but they knew her well enough to realize that her struggle was serious. "I just really wanted to get married! I was in love with the idea of marriage more than I was convinced that I had chosen the right man for me! And he just went along with the idea."

As the bride and her dad were about to walk down the aisle, her dad couldn't resist saying, "Look, sweetheart. It's not too late. Sure you want to do this? Absolutely? I'd be glad to go down the middle of the aisle by myself and announce to everyone: There won't be a wedding—so let's celebrate that. Come over to the reception and have a party with us."

Seven difficult years later, in the midst of a painful divorce, the woman still remembers her dad's line and says, "He was right. I even knew he was right! But I would have been too mortified to call things off at that point. I just remember laughing and saying, 'Oh, Dad! Always the joker!' But inside, there was this dreadful *thunk* of recognition."

they will nag you and grow louder as your wedding draws near. But if you attend to them respectfully, listening to what they have to say about you and your relationship, they will bless you with confidence and valuable insight.

Marriage in the Bible

The Bible brings together a broad spectrum of writings, histories, stories, poetry, prophecies, and letters. The first part is called the Old Testament—or the Hebrew Scriptures—and contains over forty books, composed and edited by several sources over a thousand-year period—roughly 1200 to 200 B.C.E. The New Testament—also called the Christian Scriptures—is a collection of twenty-seven books composed over a much shorter period of time, between 50 and 150 A.D. Each book reflects—and is conditioned by—the customs and assumptions of its own historical, cultural, and societal situation.

The Hebrew Scriptures

The Hebrew Scriptures say little about marriage. As a matter of fact, the Hebrew language has no single word that means "marriage." In the earlier historical periods, wealthy and high-ranking men often married several wives. (King Solomon was said to have seven hundred wives and three hundred concubines.)

Fathers arranged the marriages of their children, negotiating between themselves the terms of the nuptial contract, which included a "bride's price." The woman was given away by the father to her husband, handed over from one man to another. The primary purpose of the marriage was to produce offspring, since children were seen as necessary to a household. They helped in the fields, provided security for their parents in old age, and preserved the memory and furthered the lineage of their parents.

Love between a husband and wife was not mentioned. Most recorded marriage laws in the Hebrew Scriptures refer to a man's rights over his wife, although some few affirm her own rights. Later books—the writings of the prophets and the Song of Songs—present a more intimate understanding of marriage as a human relationship capable of reflecting a divine plan.

Given their historical and cultural situations, the writers of the Hebrew Scriptures would be unable to comprehend our contemporary understanding of marriage as a loving, affectionate, mutually respectful partnership between two equals. They did, however, provide us with a concept that over the centuries became a rich metaphor for marriage: the concept of a covenant.

God's covenant with the people is *the* recurrent theme of the Hebrew Scriptures. A covenant, like an alliance or pact, binds two parties together. It is sealed with a promise and it enumerates conditions that must be fulfilled and obligations that must be met. After the flood, God made a covenant with Noah, promising never again to destroy all living creatures by floods if Noah and his descendants would obey God. Later, God made a covenant with Abraham and Sarah, promising to make their descendants as numerous as the stars in the night sky. And through Moses God entered into a covenant at Mt. Sinai with all the people, promising to lead them into "a land flowing with milk and honey" if they would obey the terms of the covenant which were the Ten Commandments written in stone.

Although the Hebrew Scriptures' original understanding of God's relationship to the people seems formal and contractual, it is surprisingly similar to many a couple's initial understanding of their love for each other. A wedding, it would seem, shares many of the same elements of a contract or covenant: You take the initiative, you make promises, and you expect faithfulness from each other. Also, there is the often unspoken expectation of reciprocity—I'll do these things for you if you do those things for me. Upon agreement to the contract, the two people are changed: They are no longer simply two individuals, but a married couple.

At the beginning of a marriage, when you are so in love and full of hope, you don't want to think there might be problems ahead—conflicts, the need to compromise and make sacrifices, or the possibility of deeply wounding each other. But, as couples who have been married for decades know, love will always be put to the test, and sometimes you may feel you took on demands you hadn't bargained for. As time proceeds, problems may arise in the relationship. As the marriage partnership grows and develops, it becomes complicated by competing affections, differences of opinion or values. It hits snags and stumbles over bumps. It may go into a slump and need to be refreshed and re-vitalized. The love that began with mutual promises and the expectation of faithfulness needs to grow up and bloom into something more, something deeper and broader and stronger. Without growth it cannot survive the disappointments, failings, and the common human weaknesses that visit a relationship.

———

Over the centuries the writers of the Hebrew Scriptures struggled with just the same concept. Could their loving covenant with God survive their own constant mistakes? They did not have to look far for examples of the people's misconduct, and they wondered about the consequences. What happens, they asked, when the people break the terms of the agreement, when they don't abide by the rules of the covenant? At first their answer was simple and straightforward: If the people don't uphold their end of the bargain, God will cancel it. Over and over, prophets confronted the people and their rulers with harsh warnings, saying, in effect, if you continue to disobey the covenant—by worshiping false gods, for example, or oppressing the poor or making alliances with other nations—God will forsake you and leave you to the whims of your enemies. The prophets' judgments were just, fair, almost legal renderings of the terms of the covenant between God and the people.

Later prophets, however, evolved a new, more mature under-standing of love: Love is deeper than fairness. Love goes beyond the simplistic, even-trade, "tit for tat" exchange of promises and expectations of mutual fidelity. In fact, should the people break every term of their contract and prove utterly unreliable and fickle, God would continue to love them and to seek their welfare. God's main attributes, in the Hebrew Scriptures, are steadfast love and faithfulness. God loves and keeps faith, not because the people deserve or earn this love and fidelity, but simply because God cannot not be God.

The prophet Isaiah compared God's love for the Jewish people to a husband's love for his wayward wife. Even when the people (God's bride) were faithless, God stayed true. In Isaiah's time, as a result of their disobedience the people were enslaved, living in exile in Babylon. God promised through Isaiah to free them from their slavery and to restore them to the promised land:

> Yes, Yahweh has called you back like a forsaken, grief-stricken wife, like the repudiated wife of his youth, says Yahweh. "I did forsake you for a brief moment, but in a great compassion I shall take you back. In a flood of anger, for a moment I hid my face from you. But in everlasting love, I have taken pity on you. . . . I swear never to be angry with you and never to rebuke you again. For the mountains may go away and the hills may totter, but my faithful love will never leave you, my covenant of peace will never totter," says Yahweh who takes pity on you. *Isaiah 54:6–10*

Love does not excuse or overlook wrongdoing, or deny the pain it causes, but love finds within itself the strength to continue on.

———————

When you marry, you agree to expect much from each other. You vow to love each other no matter what happens, for better or worse, in sickness or in health, in full faithfulness and mutual trust, no matter what may come. You have every intention of living up to your commitment. Ideally you will always be adults; you will never disappoint each other, never waiver in your patience or your love, never be unfaithful. But the human condition is such that even good people falter, break promises, withdraw, become self-centered. We need to develop a love that is stronger and wiser than fairness, a love willing to forgive, a love that is in effect Godlike.

If the Hebrew Scriptures teach anything, they teach us the enduring steadfastness of true love.

The New Testament

In the New Testament, St. Paul's instruction about marriage (Ephesians 5:21–33) has been used throughout the centuries to justify a husband's authority over his wife, and most couples today wisely choose not to have it read at their wedding. In his own day, however, Paul's reflections would have been considered revolutionary in actually establishing a woman's dignity.

In Palestine two thousand years ago a woman had few rights. She belonged to men, first to her father and then to her husband. She could not leave her house without covering her face with a veil. She walked three paces behind her husband and did not address him in public. He could treat her as he chose, beat her if he desired, and divorce her for almost any reason and leave her destitute. She was in every way his inferior—socially, economically, and religiously.

When Paul told wives to be submissive to their husbands, he was simply reiterating the common wisdom of his day. But remarkably, he went on to tell husbands to love their wives as much as they loved themselves. Such advice might seem self-evident today, but in Paul's day such words implied a fundamental and radical reordering of values. For the first time in the Bible, someone actually said that the dynamic that bound a husband and wife was their mutual love.

The Gospels

Contrary to popular understanding, Jesus said almost nothing about marriage. Most of the time he spoke about "the reign of God" or "the kingdom of heaven." The reign of God was a vision of a more perfect world. In a more perfect world, everyone would realize that God's unconditional love and forgiveness were not far away, hard to attain, out of reach. Rather, the reign of God was at hand. It was within our grasp. It was so close and accessible that it could be touched. Every good thing was possible in the reign of God. The blind recovered their sight. Lepers were made clean. Sinners were forgiven and the estranged were reconciled. One of Jesus' favorite images for the reign of God was a wedding banquet. The wedding feast signified a special time when the normal cares and restrictions of the workday fell away. It was a grand celebration where everyone could eat and drink, dance and sing, and forget their cares for a while.

Jesus did not say anything about how a husband and wife should relate to each other, but he did lay out some very basic rules for every kind of human interaction, rules that apply especially well to marriage. Forgive each other over and over again without keeping count. Extend yourself for the other person's welfare. Don't be anxious about your physical needs, but trust in God's care. Even if the law of Moses allowed a man to divorce his wife for certain reasons—not the other way around—Jesus refused to permit divorce. In the reign of God, where all good things are possible, couples joined in marriage are united so completely and so perfectly that they can never be parted.

Jesus attended a wedding feast in Cana, where the hapless bride and groom ran out of wine. Perhaps they were poor and couldn't afford enough for all their guests. Perhaps they had planned poorly. Whatever the reason, they were sure to be embarrassed in front of their families and friends. Mary told her son about their predicament, and Jesus told the servants to fill the jars lying nearby with water and to take them to the chief steward to be tasted. These jugs normally held water used to wash the hands and feet of the guests as they arrived. It was the hospitable thing to do—provide fresh water after a dusty journey—and it was also a ritual demanded by the law of Moses. When the steward tasted the water, it had been transformed into wine. A very good wine. A wine far better than they had originally served at the feast.

For centuries Christians have pondered this simple story of Jesus' enjoyment of a wedding feast and his affection for the couple. They have seen in it as sign of Jesus' approval and blessing of marriage. And they have understood it as a parable of how Jesus turns the ordinary into the extraordinary. In any case, persons entering their own marriages will certainly come upon times when things have gone flat or where the relationship has become ordinary and humdrum. Then they can remember this story, where the ordinary, brought before the Lord, is charged with the Spirit. Where the ordinary is quickened and brought to life. Where the mundane is the source of the ecstatic.

Praying Together

If you are not in the habit of praying, this is a good time to begin. The cultivation of prayer is a way to slowly build and
strengthen your spiritual life. A life in the Spirit needs some cultivation. Nothing elaborate or complicated. Nothing awkward
or hard to do. But ignored and forgotten, the life of the spirit
withers, and we feel estranged from God and from God's love
for us.

If prayer is a way of having an intimate conversation with
God, you may feel defeated before you begin. You may think
you are inadequate before God, not knowing what to say or do.
So, go ahead! Feel small and inadequate. Be tongue-tied or

speechless. No need to get bogged down wondering what you believe or don't believe. Even knowing our inadequacies is a good beginning. Simply stand there before this God who loves you. Collect yourself. And ask to be in a right alignment with this holy mystery that surrounds all things.

The inner life of prayer appreciates even our smallest efforts. Slowly we develop a habit of standing before God, this God who gave us life and gave us one another. Slowly we discover we want to return God's love for us in the way we live and love one another. We begin to seek signs of God and, in fact, discover that God is not far away and out of reach. We find God revealed in one another, in the ordinary moments that make up our days.

Praying Alone

There are many ways to pray. We can take time to sit quietly by ourselves, aware that we have placed ourselves in God's presence. We can ask for help, for guidance, for wisdom, for peace of mind, for a way to live this life. We can express our thankfulness and praise for the joys and mysteries of life. Or we can simply place ourselves there in silence, breathing in and breathing out, aware that God is our life's breath and the heart of our being.

We can look for a sacred text, take Scripture passages or a book of prayers and meditations to act as a guide. But we can also seek a more direct experience of God. We can pray as we walk down the streets of the city, sit in a bus or subway, and see God's reflection in the eyes of those who pass. We can pray when we run. When we walk the beach. When we work or play in God's nature. We can pray at work, dedicating it to the glory of God as we move through the tasks of the day.

Certain postures and gestures contribute to our prayer by placing our bodies in a position that best expresses our attitude. We can stand tall and at attention when we are listening to or praising God. We might kneel in an attitude of adoration or, at other times, when we feel small and in need or afraid. We can sit on the floor, legs crossed, back straight, eyes closed, hands open in reception. We can speak memorized words or speak freely from the heart, cross ourselves or fold our hands. Gestures are a part of prayer and an aid to it, but they are not always necessary. We can pray anywhere at any time in any way our hearts move us.

It is helpful to create a quiet corner in your apartment or house where you can always go to pray. Some people find it helpful to light a candle or incense—the energy and movement of a flame and curling, fragrant smoke contribute to prayer and praise.

EARLY ON, we created a little prayer table in the alcove in our hall. A straight-backed chair is next to it. A small carpet on the floor before it. We have a book stand with a book opened to readings that speak of the season. We framed a series of interchangeable icons and classic religious reproductions which we hang on the wall. We light a lamp in a flameproof glass and keep it burning for important intentions. One year we added a dish of river pebbles to burn our incense in. As the kids came and grew, they began to go there spontaneously, bringing the first dandelions in spring, writing their petitions on slips of paper and putting them there, drawing pictures of Nona when she was sick in the hospital, cutting out pictures from the papers of situations that disturbed them—starving children, or a flooded house. Having a place to pray, alone or together, a place to literally put our concerns, helped make praying a habit in the house.

Praying Together

Prayer, of course, is not just a personal thing, something we do alone. Something powerful happens when we dare to share our prayers. A couple, praying together, are likely to grow closer together. By praying together we open ourselves to a new level of intimacy. We lay our hearts open to God when we pray, but we also lay ourselves open to each other in a whole new way. To be willing to pray together is to trust each other.

As you've been preparing yourselves for your marriage, you have probably been talking about a range of issues, conflicts, values, and hopes that you may have found difficult to discuss. Many couples have the greatest difficulty discussing their faith lives— not just what they believe or wonder about, but how they practice what they believe and how they pray. They feel vulnerable and awkward when they share their hearts in this way. As a result, they never come around to forming a spiritual life within the context of their marriage. They find it difficult to sustain their prayers even as a private undertaking. So, commonly, they wait until something dramatic happens in their lives to jolt them into retrieving a life of prayer and remind them of their need for God.

The easiest way to begin sharing your prayers is with simple gestures. Grasp hands. Bow your heads. Collect yourselves until your breathing is even and the inner noise of anxiety has stopped. You do not need to speak aloud, not until you are ready—maybe not at all. Do this for a few moments before you part in the morning. Bless one another by simply putting your hand lightly on the other's head.

Saying grace before meals is another easy way to begin. The

bustle of getting a meal ready has finally stopped. You are brought together at the table. With the good smells of food in front of you, you pause, catch your breath, look at each other, and know that the food before you is a gift. Sharing your meal brings you back into relationship. Take each other by the hand and say a brief prayer. Thank God for providing you with all the good things that sustain you and, mindful of those in need, ask God's blessings on them. Recite a grace you memorized as a child, if you wish, or be spontaneous. Mention, perhaps, the names of people you are concerned about or your unresolved problems and worries. Prayer can be as simple as that.

Church is not the only place to pray; it is a holy place where the larger family gathers to pray. If you are both from the same religious tradition, you may already be attending church together. If you are from different traditions, don't "compromise" by giving up both traditions. You could alternate: On one Sunday go to one church and on the next Sunday go to the other. Afterward, maybe over breakfast, talk to each other about the experience. As long as you are sensitive and respectful, you can ask any question you want about each other's beliefs or practices. Attending church services isn't only about being wafted up into some religious experience—which isn't very likely to happen! It is also about bringing the experiences of the week to the house of the Lord and asking that they be blessed. It is about praising God. It is about gathering as a larger family and resetting our values, our commitments, our goals, and our responsibilities to this community of faith.

Prayer is also a way to observe the natural rhythm of time. It is based on the rhythms of light and darkness, of waking and sleeping, of working and resting. Between the birth of the new day and its dying lies our work and our play, our struggles and endeavors, fate and fertility, growth and perils. Without prayer to frame the day's birth and its dying, the day lacks meaning and form. So also the week. When Sunday comes, put your work aside. Make it a day for praise and for relaxing together.

———

As you prepare for your wedding, take a moment here and there to pray together. It can help you maintain your perspective and confirm your values. Pray for the grace to let what is important be important and let the minor details remain minor.

Here are two prayers you can recite to keep you focused on what matters:

> *Gracious God,*
> *we thank you for the love you share with us*
> *in and through each other.*
> *As we draw nearer to the day*
> *when we will be made one in marriage,*
> *we ask that you turn each of our plans,*
> *our worries and concerns,*
> *into a means of drawing closer together in love.*
> *Bless us, our families and friends.*
> *Bless, too, our hopes and dreams.*
> *May all we do begin with your inspiration*
> *and continue through to a happy conclusion*
> *under the guidance of your wisdom.*
> *Amen.*

Remind us, Lord, today and every day that
love is patient and kind.
It envies no one.
It does not seek its own interests.
It is slow to anger and quick to forgive.
To love is not to brood over hurt feelings.
Remind us, Lord, when we grow weary or tense that
you are our strength and our refuge,
the source of our joy.
As these days grow hectic,
remind us that it is a holy married life we are preparing for
and that our wedding day is only that: a day.
And help us remember that the whole day of our wedding
is more important than any one of its details.
Finally, fix it into our hearts, Lord, that
only three things matter:
faith, hope, and love,
and the greatest of these is love.
Amen.

And as you begin your married life together, you can make it a habit to pray these prayers:

Love takes to itself the life of the loved one.
The greater our love,
the greater the sensitivity of our souls.
The fuller our love,
the fuller our knowledge of God.
The more ardent our love,
the more fervent our prayer.

The more perfect our love,
the holier the life we lead.

From Colossians 3:12–15

Because, O God, we are your chosen ones,
clothe us with heartfelt mercy,
with kindness, humility,
meekness, and patience.
Help us bear with one another;
and forgive whatever grievances we have against one another.
May we forgive as you, O Lord, have forgiven us.
Over all these virtues, teach us to love,
with that love which binds the rest together
and makes them perfect.
Let peace reign in our hearts,
since you have called us, as members of the one body, to that
  peace.
Dedicate us to thankfulness.
Amen.

Praying is a discipline for the good health of the spirit just as exercise and nutrition are disciplines for a healthy body. Praying is a habit to cultivate.

5

Making the Day: Examples

Pam and Javier's Wedding

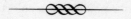

I received a map to the church and the reception hall along with a note explaining that the couple considered my presence at their wedding gift enough and would I please not buy anything for them. I appreciated the map and the sentiment, but I was perplexed since I hadn't received an invitation. It arrived two weeks later. "My father was in charge of the invitations," the bride explained, "and since I didn't entirely trust him to mail them out in time, I sent the maps as a way of giving people advance notice." Pam was a research chemist who worked with the church's youth group. She organized the group's social outreach activities (visiting a retirement home and serving meals at a home for runaway teens). Javier, a fireman, was also involved with the church. He organized its youth softball league. The people most active in the church all knew and loved Pam and Javier.

Pam was twenty-eight, Javier was thirty-two, and I couldn't imagine a couple less suited to a frilly or formal wedding. Knowing the two of them and from the tone of their invitation, I knew from the beginning that this was going to be a different kind of wedding, certainly informal, but friendly and relaxed.

A note on the map warned that I might have difficulty finding parking, so I arrived early. People were already gathering at the door of the church, a small, low-roofed cinder-block building. The bride and groom mingled among the guests at the entrance, greeting people, introducing them to one another, and asking them to find themselves a seat. In the seven years I had known Pam I can't remember ever having seen her wear a dress. I half expected to see her dressed as I best knew her—in jeans and a T-shirt. But she looked radiant in a colorful dress. A friend had made it for her the previous week. Javier wore black slacks, a white collarless shirt, and a vest made of the same fabric as Pam's dress.

Apparently, at the urging of a girlfriend, Pam had in fact submitted herself to trying on a few wedding dresses, but the experience had sent them both into hysterics. One look in the mirror, and they both agreed nothing on the racks was going to work for her.

The church itself was simple. It had a short single aisle with pews off to both sides. It could accommodate fewer than two hundred people. Although there was only one bouquet of flowers in the entire church, the place felt festive. Taking their cue from Pam and Javier, the guests were dressed casually, and they chatted with other guests. It was as if their friendliness and warmth were decoration enough for the church. The person sitting next to me introduced himself at once, and we started talking. From the moment I arrived, it seemed as if I were attending a family reunion.

Four musicians in the front of the church (three singers and a pianist) stood off to the side. One of them caught our attention and welcomed us. "In order to make this truly a celebration of Javier's and Pam's love," she said, "please join with us in singing." She then announced the opening hymn, told us where to find it in the hymnal, and asked us to stand.

We sang what could be called only, I guess, a contemporary hymn as the procession began. A woman walked in carrying a lectionary raised high. Pam and Javier followed close behind, walking hand in hand, and behind them the priest. When they approached the sanctuary, they fanned out in front of the altar and paused briefly. The woman walked to the pulpit and placed the book down. Javier and Pam walked to the side of the altar, where two seats had been set opposite the musicians. The priest bowed to the altar, went behind it, and kissed it in a sign of reverence. He faced us. When the last verse of the hymn ended, he made the sign of the cross and greeted us with the standard greeting: "The grace and peace of our Lord Jesus Christ, the love of God, and the fellowship of the Holy Spirit be with you all." We responded, "And also with you." Judging by the response, I estimate that at least three quarters of the people present were familiar with the Catholic order of worship.

Javier then addressed the people, saying simply how happy and honored he felt that we had come from so many different places and some of us from so far away to join them. "This isn't just a celebration of our love," Pam added. "It's a community's celebration. We wouldn't be here without your guidance and example. And we can do this only with your support." The priest then asked us to bow our heads in prayer. After a brief silence he voiced a prayer. We said "Amen," and he asked us to be seated for the readings.

The woman who had processed in with the book stood from her place in the congregation, came forward to the altar, and bowed her head slightly to honor it. She walked to the pulpit, opened the book, looked up at us, and said, "A reading from the Song of Songs." She had obviously rehearsed the reading, because she proclaimed it in such a way that its poetry and beauty touched us all. She paused briefly at the end of the passage before saying, "The word of the Lord." We responded, "Thanks be to God."

There was a long silence, maybe a minute's worth, an intentional silence that actually let us think about the words we had just heard.

One of the singers stood up, asked us to join in singing a psalm, and told us where to find it in the music books.

A man rose from his place in the congregation and approached the pulpit in much the same way as the previous reader. He, too, found his place in the book, looked at us, and said, "A reading from Paul's First Letter to the Corinthians." Although I had heard Paul's description of love ("Love is patient, love is kind . . .") so many times I could almost recite it by heart, this man proclaimed it simply and powerfully. It is such a rich description of love—deep, insightful, and not at all sentimental—that I don't at all mind hearing it again and again. He paused at the end of the passage and said, "The word of the Lord."

This time there was a briefer moment of silence before all four musicians stood and together motioned for us to stand too. They sang a familiar setting of "Alleluia" and most of us spontaneously joined in.

The priest approached the pulpit. He extend his hands as if in blessing toward us and said, "The Lord be with you." We answered, "And also with you." "A reading from the holy Gospel according to John," he said, and we answered, "Thanks be to God." He then read the passage about the wedding feast at Cana in Galilee, where Jesus turned water into wine, but he did so in a way that made it sound as if he were telling a story. At the end of it he paused and said, "The Gospel of the Lord." We answered, "Praise to you, Lord Jesus Christ."

We sat and he began preaching. We laughed at his story of how Pam and Javier had met; it captured the spirit of both of them. And then he explained how he had seen God's grace work in and through them, turning the water of their daily lives into a wine that brought joy to others.

After finishing his homily, he turned to the couple and asked them to come forward with their witnesses. Javier's brother stood by his side and Pam's best friend stood by hers. Only then did I realize that she wasn't carrying a bouquet of any sort. The priest asked the couple three questions about their freedom and willingness to enter into matrimony.

The priest then addressed the congregation. "Marriage is not a private endeavor," he said, "but a social and religious undertaking. This couple could not have come to this place in their lives on their own. They can't strengthen and preserve the unity they celebrate today without your continued love. And so I ask you, 'Do you promise to nurture and support Pam and Javier with your example, encouragement, and prayers?' " We all answered, "We do."

He turned back to the couple. "In the presence of God, this faith community, your family and friends, and with our pledge of support, please state your intentions."

They spoke the traditional Catholic wedding vow, repeating it after the priest, speaking it to each other, but loud enough for all of us to hear.

Javier's brother handed the priest two rings, which he blessed with holy water. Placing a ring on Javier's finger, Pam said, "Javier, take this ring as a sign of my love and fidelity, in the name of the Father and of the Son and of the Holy Spirit." Javier said the same.

The bride and groom kissed and we all spontaneously burst into applause. The priest then said to all of us, "Please share with each other some sign of Christ's peace." That was all the excuse people needed to start hugging one another. Pam and Javier were surrounded by well-wishers, but they managed to greet just about everyone in the church. And I realized the truth of the priest's words about how they were like wine that brought joy to other people's hearts.

Throughout the ceremony people popped up from their seats or leaned into the aisle to snap photographs the spontaneous way people do at informal gatherings, but no professional photographer intruded in the flow of events.

The priest regained our attention and asked us to extend our right hand in blessing toward the couple while the musicians sang a song of blessing. The refrain was repeated a number of times, and soon we were all joining in.

The priest invited us to pray. Pam's father came forward and read a series of petitions—asking for blessings on the newly married couple, for blessings on all married couples and families, for blessings on those people (some were living and some were dead) who could not be with us this day—and concluded each petition with "Let us pray to the Lord." We responded, "Lord, hear our prayer." Finally the priest concluded with a prayer.

The two mothers brought forward bread and wine, and the ceremony continued with a traditional Catholic Mass. At communion time, the priest invited everyone to come forward. "If you are not able to receive communion," he said, "cross your hands in front of your chest, and I will give you a blessing."

At the conclusion of the entire celebration Pam invited us all to the reception which was at the YMCA three blocks away. She said that she and Javier were walking there and we were welcome to join them.

We sang a hymn as the couple processed out, followed by their witnesses and the priest and finally by the rest of us.

The youth group had decorated the gym at the Y, setting up tables along one side and creating a dance floor on the other side. Javier's team had organized the meal—tapas, paella, salad, and sangria. There was eating and drinking and dancing and toasts (led by Pam) and roasts (led by the president of the parish council). Some of guests were from the nursing home, and a few from the teen center. No one, actually, acted like a guest. It felt as if everyone belonged, as if everyone were part of the party.

Jill and Ed's Wedding

It's always tricky when the bride and groom grew up and have family and friends in different corners of the country and now, as adults, they live in a third place. Where should they hold the wedding?

My friends, Jill and Ed, settled the question by going to Jill's hometown to marry where, in fact, they first met at the college and where a few mutual friends still live. They themselves haven't been living there for the past two and a half years.

Jill is Episcopalian and Ed grew up Lutheran. Neither one is currently connected with a church, but both were committed to being married in a church ceremony. They spoke with the new

Episcopal minister at the parish Jill's parents attended and with the Lutheran campus minister. Both of the clergy agreed that the wedding should be celebrated at the Episcopal parish, and the Lutheran minister offered to give them their premarriage counseling and to be part of the wedding ceremony. A real ecumenical ceremony it was.

The Episcopal church was this pretty little stone structure on a grassy rise in the middle of the town. It had a bell tower, a community hall, a central courtyard, kitchens, offices, and the church itself. It wasn't a huge church. I'd say it was rather small—or it seemed small. The inside was oak—dark. Peaceful and beautiful. I think it must have been built in the early 1800s.

There wasn't a hint of rain that day. It was bright and sunny, and because it was spring the grounds around the church were filled with blooming dogwood trees and magnolias. The wedding was to begin at noon. The guests parked at the lot across the road and found their way into the courtyard, where the main entry to the church was trimmed with flowers and ferns. In the doorway, both Jill's and Ed's parents and brothers and sisters met us, introduced us to others, and took us to our places in the church. It was comforting for me to see both Jill's stepdad and her biological dad (whom I'd never met before) present and cheerfully functioning within a few feet of each other! I've never been ushered at a wedding by a pretty young woman before, but it was Ed's younger sister who took us to our pew. There was a lot of happy chattering at the doorway as people were welcomed, introduced, and led into the church. The two families were gracious hosts to us right from the start.

The church was dark and cool. Patches of colored light from the windows stained the floor and walls and people's faces. At each seat there were leaflets for us with an outline of the service and some prayers that we were going to recite together. I looked over the music—there would be organ music. No solos. And just then a quartet—two flutes, a violin, and a viola—were playing chamber music. A single large bouquet stood behind the altar, and small sprays of flowers and greens marked off the front pews for the families.

The church filled up rapidly. I liked the fact that it wasn't a cavernous place and that we all had to be packed in pretty tight. I liked recognizing some of the faces from years ago—nodding a greeting before they settled in.

The quartet came to the end of a piece and stopped playing. Everyone shifted and looked around. And when all the shifting around stopped, with a blast of the organ and a trumpet a man processed down the aisle with a cross, followed by two young fellows carrying candles. The crossbearer was Jill's elder step-brother, and the boys were Ed's nephews. Behind them came Jill's favorite aunt carrying the book aloft. The Lutheran pastor and the Episcopal rector, fully vested and walking side by side, followed the book. Then came a whole cluster of beautiful kids, boys and girls from ages maybe two into their teens, all dressed up and each carrying a single flower. I figured out that Jill's relatives carried a calla lily and Ed's relatives carried a spike of del-phinium. Then right behind them came Ed's brothers and sister in a little cluster. Then came seven grandparents in a group! And then there came Ed. He walked between his parents, and they were holding hands. Already there were tears. There followed Jill's two sisters and a brother. Behind them, Jill's dad and his wife. Then, right behind them came Jill, radiantly beautiful be-tween her mother and stepfather.

It was grand! What a start. I'd never seen a procession like that for a wedding. It occurred to me only much later that for all the formality and grandness—the priests were vested and the two acolytes too—there were no tuxes and the rest of the people in the party wore colors that ranged between light blue into deep lavenders—the women, that is. The boys and the men all wore blazers and white shirts. And all the little girls wore white dresses in various styles. There was a basket at each side of the sanctuary entry and the children who were carrying flowers put them in there among ferns.

The crossbearer, the acolytes, and the two ministers entered the sanctuary and turned toward the people and waited. All the children peeled off on either side, went around to the side, and took their places in their pews. Then the two families turned and faced one another and presented Jill and Ed to each other. The two went up into the sanctuary. One sister and one brother followed as witnesses. The woman who was carrying the book brought it up to the table and bowed and took her place at the side, where the acolytes and the crossbearer—after planting the cross in its stand—also sat.

All the other adults went around the side and entered their pews. Some of them sat in among the kids, obviously their children. Then the two ministers addressed the whole church with a wonderful, resounding welcome prayer. The rest of the ceremony was clear and clean and simple. The aunt was a really good reader and the second reading was done by one of Ed's brothers—his voice was a little weak maybe. The Episcopal rector read the Gospel. The Lutheran minister gave a sermon. It was based on nine points which, in fact, he had written up on a card and gave the couple as a wedding gift.

At one point there were special blessings or petitions for the bride and groom and all these different people from among the guests stood up and read them out. The last one was read by Ed's father, and he read it so slowly and strongly and clearly! He was better than all the other readers put together. There was also a blessing that we all said together, raising our hands out over the couple in blessing. That blessing was written in our folder. They didn't do the schmaltzy kiss routine, but the ministers said to us: "The peace of the Lord be always with you." They offered one another an embrace, and each kissed the bride and groom. Then the bride and groom embraced and kissed and then they kissed their witnesses and then all four of them came down from the sanctuary and sent their hugs into the congregation and it just spread out among the people—you just caught the spirit and sent it on.

When the ceremony came to an end and it was time to go, the organ and the trumpet pealed out with "Joyful, Joyful We Adore Thee." Magnificent. It's music that just gets you in the core of your being. A few people knew the words and began to sing aloud—and very well, I might add—and that made people spontaneously hum and sing along. We all left the church singing and humming and outside, in the courtyard, the church bells were ringing out! Jill and Ed were standing there in the middle of the yard and all the kids and a few of their parents had gathered around them and were whirling around them in a circle so that we all joined in. The two were a picture. The whole thing was a picture!

Jill was stunning. How many times did I hear that day "regal looking." Her hair was caught up in a twist, she had a wreath of tiny white flowers on her head, and her veil billowed out like a sail all around her. Her dress was elegant—very simple—not all done up in beads or lace—very tasteful. Ed is drop-dead handsome. And so expressive. There he stood, beaming, with one arm around his beautiful Jill.

The tables in the hall were set up with fabulous food which we took out into the sunshine and ate at little tables placed around the outer edges of a dance floor. It wasn't long before the suit jackets and blazers were shed. Everyone was now dancing to loud, mad music. Collars were loosened. Some of the women gradually kicked off their shoes. The band was good and the music was easy to dance to for all age groups. The kids danced with one another and dashed around finding their own games among the adults and ran around the grassy slopes. What is it about white dresses in the sunshine on fresh green lawns!

Some of the other details I found to be thoughtful: There was very little evidence of photography going on—at least they were pretty subtle. And my guess is that the party posed for pictures before the guests arrived. No one threw rice or birdseed, but they did have some baskets of streamers on little sticks to wave when Jill and Ed got into their car.

Did anything go wrong? Well, from my perspective as a guest, I couldn't see that anything went wrong. I heard the guest book got lost for a week, but the maintenance people found it and brought it to the church office. One of the toasts offered was a little long and windy, I thought. I noticed that after a while the older folks went inside, out of the sun and away from the music. It was too loud for them. Some of the teens—oh, yes!—decorated *the wrong car*—which actually was a great laugh, because it belonged to a fellow who brought a girlfriend and their relationship was very new and tenuous. They had to ride through town all done up in streamers and get honked at by the world, who mistook them for newlyweds.

I know that Ed and Jill repaired to a nearby hotel, where they were still so jazzed by the experience and so hungry—they never stopped long enough to eat at their own reception—that they did their post mortem over a good dinner.

Certainly, it all seemed to end too soon. Probably because it was such a fine celebration.

Peg and Larry's Wedding

Peg and Larry met in graduate school. Peg is an architect and Larry teaches biology. They are the kind of people who gather friends around them without effort.

Peg bought a bungalow a few years ago in what she likes to call a recovering part of town. The house has a classic front porch, hardwood floors, a built-in buffet with leaded glass doors, and a stained glass window on the landing. It needed a lot of work—a *lot* of work—but she bravely took it on. She and Larry proceeded to work their tails off restoring it. They put in new plumbing in the kitchen but saved things like the old sink. A lot of us spent time there on weekends, helping—stripping paint, puttying windows, sanding and sealing the floors. We got a kick out of entertaining Peg's little Hannah, who is a precocious eight-year-old. And, of course, we loved the beer and pizza.

We teased them that if they survived "this old house," they ought to celebrate by getting married. Well, that's actually what happened. They put in a wonderful garden. Larry can grow anything, and I think when he's had it with plumbing or rewiring, he escapes into the garden for a change of pace.

Peg designed and built a beautiful arbor over which they eventually want to grow grapes, but for the wedding it was the focal point. There were no chairs. We stood in a half circle in the grass around the arbor. Peg stood on one side of the garden with her mother (Peg's dad died when she was in high school), her sister, Netty, and a beaming Hannah. Larry stood on the other side with his mom and dad and two brothers. They waited there on both sides of the arbor until the minister appeared, and then the musician stopped playing her flute. The minister called the two of them to come stand on either side of her. I liked that—that we didn't have to look at the backs of them the whole time. I read the first reading—the one about creation, about how man and woman need each other. Another friend read a second reading— also from the Bible, I believe—but it was poetic and rather erotic. She read well.

The minister read the story about Jesus turning water into wine at a wedding and gave a good short sermon about the art of transforming the everyday, ordinary things into something special and effervescent, like Jesus did with the water, and like Peg and Larry did making their fixer-upper house into a thing of beauty. And she said that married people—all people, really—

shouldn't take anything for granted because with reverence and the right spirit we can all learn the art of transforming the dull into the spectacular.

A woman sang a song and I could have done without that. She was a bit operatic and it didn't feel that it fit. But I believe she was Larry's aunt or some relative. Then Netty read an excellent poem she wrote about growing up with Peg as the perfectly ac-complished older sister, memories, little-sister perceptions, funny stories. She wove the importance of Hannah in the mix and captured her personality completely. You know, sometimes we roared with laughter and then we were all dabbing our eyes, but it wasn't a bit sentimental. It fit in well, her poem, because it was separated from the Bible readings. She even read it from the other side of the arbor. It didn't compete, you might say.

They said the traditional vows, during which Larry's brother and Netty stepped forward as witnesses. But then—a very nice thing—the minister invited Hannah to stand next to her and hold the rings as she prayed a blessing over them. In the blessing she called on the Holy Spirit to bring special gifts down on these rings, this sign of their love and fidelity.

The minister then turned to all of us. She told us that we had just heard Peg and Larry pledge their love and faithfulness to each other, but did we, as a community of friends, also pledge our faithfulness to them? Would we stand by them no matter the joys or hardships that would come their way? Did we stand by Hannah as her honorary aunts and uncles? She told us that just as Peg and Larry couldn't have restored the house without us, they couldn't polish and perfect their relationship without us. I don't remember ever being asked to make my own vows of friendship and support at a wedding, but it was a true opportunity for us to say our own "I do" in support of these good friends whom we all loved.

The sky got dark—it threatened to rain all the while we were gathered in the garden—and after the minister pronounced them husband and wife, there was—as if on cue!—a clap of thunder, and it began to pour! It was a riot. We all clapped and then everyone dashed inside through the kitchen door. Two women from the neighborhood who acted as caterers had taken all the dishes we'd brought—did I mention this was all potluck?—and set them out on the dining room table. They provided a smoked salmon and a turkey. As we stood around, the minister said she didn't think that a clap of thunder was quite good enough to close a wedding rite, so she ended it by teaching us all a sung blessing. She showed us how to sing it over Peg and Larry and then how to share it with the people around us. It was accompanied by some simple gestures, and you were supposed to go around in two concentric circles and really look into the eyes of each person as you came to them. It was very moving! Then she led us in a thoughtful grace. And we ate.

I have to add here that I wouldn't have guessed that a rained-out garden wedding could have such a truly unifying, deeply moving, and spiritual aspect to it. I credit the skill and the genuine reverence of that minister for pulling it off. I didn't know how much the biblical language would bring to the ceremony. It added a depth that contemporary readings could not have. But the minister also knew how to pace things. She allowed long periods of silence. She didn't joke with us, even though she was never even slightly pompous. She also had a way of both recognizing and verbalizing the kind of friends we were and the kind of community we could be. I believe we were all struck by that.

The food was great! Everybody actually found a flat space to sit—like all the way up the stairway or out on the porch. And when it was time for toasts, Peg's mother gave a nice, strong toast and Larry's mom gave one also. I thought that was very unusual, and effective. After toasting—and because we were all in there facing one direction—Larry thought it would be good to cut the cake and he did a spontaneous thing: He said that all his comrades over the long time that he and Peg were restoring the house had taught him a lot about friendship, patience, craftsmanship, but the best part was the cooperation and teamwork. He'd learned not only to be part of a team with some of us, but he'd also become a very solid team with Peg, secure in the process of sharing their differing gifts and viewpoints. He said they wanted to feed each other a piece of cake in honor of all the ways they nourished and shared with each other, and he wanted each of us to come up, get our cake, and then find three other people to go and share that cake with—one could be someone we knew, but the other two had to be someone we just met. It made for a lot of milling around and mixing.

We danced out on the porch. Someone had put together a good collection of dance tapes. It was pretty crowded, but I think that was part of the fun.

Now, I need to mention that some people have taken to opening wedding gifts in front of everyone, and I think that's really tacky, actually. How many toasters do you want to open up in a row and go into raptures about? So as a rule, I think it's a very crummy idea. But a bunch of us who stayed on actually came around to begging Peg and Larry to open theirs, because they had asked for gifts of old period things for the house which we might find in junk shops or flea markets. We'd all been so much part of the renovations and had learned so much about that style that we were dying to see what others had brought. One of the really fabulous things was for their chandelier in the dining room. A friend who does glass blowing made them a set of contemporary in-the-spirit-of-Tiffany lamps to replace what had been lost long ago. Perfect. There were quite a number of porcelain doorknobs. Brass kitchen pulls. A great set of forties tablecloths. One of those rounded, squat toasters that still worked. Anyhow, that was fun. It was all fun. And we finally had to go home under a relay of umbrellas to our cars.

Oh! And by the way: We're buying the bungalow four doors down. We like the neighbors!

A Blessing

May every blessing and grace be yours.

May your love grow stronger and deeper with each passing year.

May joy and delight fill your home.

May daily problems not vex you unduly

nor the desire for earthly possessions dominate your lives.

If you have children, may they return your love many times over.

May you have true friends to stay by you in joy and in sorrow.

With wise and generous hearts,

may you help all who come to you in need of comfort.

And may you reach a ripe old age together,

content for having lived a life of goodness and worth.

INDEX

GERTRUD MUELLER NELSON is known internationally as an illustrator, author, and speaker. Her books, *To Dance With God* and *Here All Dwell Free,* have won her a wide following.

CHRISTOPHER WITT is coauthor of *From Loneliness to Love.* He has published articles and produced tapes on recovery from divorce and other losses, and he is a sought-after teacher, retreat director, and speaker.

Both live in San Diego.